What people are saying about …

THE WAY OF BLESSING

'Roy Godwin's story has impacted many thousands of lives and, in *The Way of Blessing*, he invites us all to carry the blessing of God out into the world to transform communities'.

Pete Greig, author of *Red Moon Rising* and *God on Mute*

'I read Roy's first book, *The Grace Outpouring*, in 2011 and that book literally sparked a chain reaction of events that led to my church purchasing the iconic Bible College of Wales in Swansea and Pisgah Chapel in Loughor. So I am cautious about reading books by Roy because they will spark something prophetic in you and bring you down a path less trodden, but full of adventure. Roy's book, *The Way of Blessing*, will surely encourage you to action. Be warned'.

Rev. Yang Tuck Yoong, senior pastor at Cornerstone Community Church, Singapore

'We live in a truly tumultuous and dangerous time in the history of our world. Nations are warring against nations. Our natural reaction as Christians is that we want and need to pray. The big question is how? How should we pray for the Middle East and Africa? How do we pray into closed nations and for those who are enduring acute persecution? How do we pray for a world that is increasingly interconnected and therefore vulnerable to terrorism and environmental catastrophes? This book has been hugely instrumental in refocusing and reshaping my own prayer life, as has my personal friendship with the author. If you need help and encouragement in developing your prayer life, then look no further than *The Way of Blessing*'.

Eddie Lyle, president of Open Doors UK & Ireland

'*The Way of Blessing* continues as a significant contribution in the exploration of what God can and does do when our focus is upon blessing: God's blessing of us and our blessing of those with whom we come into contact. We are drawn into the lives of those who come seeking and receive blessing through their stories; we are encouraged to explore what God is doing and how we can cooperate with God's desire to bless as part of God's Mission purpose. This book challenges God's Church to be places of blessing founded upon how God has blessed his Church. With its focus on praying blessing, it gives us a way in which we can enter into the Mission of God which is available to us all—young and old. This is material that I want everyone in the Diocese of Willochra to have access to'.

The Rt. Rev. John Stead, bishop of Willochra, Australia

'Roy Godwin continues the story of God's beautiful work in and through the community of Ffald y Brenin, as the Grace Outpouring turns to a flood of Blessing, which is impacting God's world. In the midst of it are Roy Godwin and Daphne, ordinary self-effacing Christians who simply desire to honour and worship the living God and to throw away anything that hinders the full flow of His love, mercy, blessing, and healing. Writing rooted in the deep reality of ordinary Christian lives, and at times painfully honest, but much more significantly rooted in the reality of the Father's profound love, to read this book is to step into the Way of Blessing. The way of God's redemptive salvation in all its aspects, as that Blessing pours from every page. Read, be blessed, worship the Lord, and join many, many others in being a minister of God's blessing in and through the great name of Jesus'.

Eric Kyte, vicar of St. John the
Evangelist, Roslyn, New Zealand

the WAY of BLESSING

the WAY of BLESSING

STEPPING INTO THE MISSION AND PRESENCE OF GOD

ROY GODWIN

WITH DAVE ROBERTS

David C Cook®
transforming lives together

THE WAY OF BLESSING
Published by David C Cook
4050 Lee Vance View
Colorado Springs, CO 80918 U.S.A.

David C Cook U.K., Kingsway Communications
Eastbourne, East Sussex BN23 6NT, England

The graphic circle C logo is a registered trademark of David C Cook.

The website addresses recommended throughout this book are offered as a
resource to you. These websites are not intended in any way to be or imply an
endorsement on the part of David C Cook, nor do we vouch for their content.

LCCN 2016933803
ISBN 978-0-7814-1442-5
eISBN 978-0-7814-1433-3

The Team: Kyle Duncan, Ian Matthews, Amy Konyndyk, Nick Lee, Susan Murdock
Cover Design: Jon Middel
Cover Photo: iStock

Printed and bound by CPI Group (UK) Ltd, Croydon, CR0 4YY
First Edition 2016

2 3 4 5 6 7 8 9 10

052616

In memory of—and with thanks to—the anonymous, illiterate rural preacher who led me to the Lord.

CONTENTS

ACKNOWLEDGEMENTS

Without the blessing of many others into my life this book could never have been written. To the growing team at Ffald y Brenin who thrill me by their passion for the Lord, their servant hearts and their amazing commitment to serving the purposes of God through Ffald y Brenin. Thank you!

To Bishop Saunders Davies who lives so richly in what he preaches and has enriched me. Thank you!

To that procession of godly men who have befriended, mentored, helped, and inspired me over the years. Thank you!

I need to thank Dave Roberts, not only for his craftsmanship in helping to shape and put my words into printable form, but also for our many discussions which have so often helped me to clarify my own thinking. Iron sharpens iron. Thank you!

And last but by no means least, to Daphne, who has once again had to put up with my absence while I have been writing, even when I have been present! Daphne, you know what I mean. Thank you!

The Way of Blessing

We seek rhythms of life that will nurture truth within us.

We are nurtured by the compassion of the Father
We believe that He has crowned us with love and compassion.

We embrace a salvation that touches every part of our lives
We believe that He is present to us now, with the power to heal, wisdom for our circumstance and with outrageous grace for our forgiveness.

We desire instructed hearts and minds
We seek rhythms of life that will nurture truth within us.

We want to be carriers of His presence
We long for the manifest presence of God to go
with us.

We are forerunners of the blessing of God
We want to be those whose words nourish many.

We seek to imitate Jesus
We believe greater things are yet to come.

**We believe that blessing for others us, and
others, is nurtured by community**
We want to be known as a people that have God
with us.

INTRODUCTION

We would like to tell you a story. It's a story of the love of God at work to forgive, heal and empower. As we have walked through this story, awestruck by the mercy of God, the work of Jesus and the miraculous work of the Spirit today, we know that God has *instructed our hearts and our tongues* that we might say the words that sustain, instruct, heal and bring deliverance to those we encounter. We want to share what He has taught us.

We have woven the story of the Way of Blessing using the threads of grace that we have seen at work in our lives. The picture is not really complete without all the threads. We note that the scripture often reminds us that the work of God in our lives often finds expression in diverse ways and in that diversity we find strength. God instructs our hearts, shapes our character and spurs us into action in many ways.

Those who are described as blessed in the Sermon on the Mount are hungry, pure in spirit, merciful, humble, peace-making and sympathetic. Those who know the Spirit at work in their lives will see character change that will include love, joy, peace, forbearance, kindness, goodness, faithfulness, gentleness and self-control. Those who listen for the voice of God will receive messages of wisdom, messages of knowledge, faith, gifts of healing, miraculous powers, prophecy, distinguishing between spirits, speaking in different kinds of tongues, and the interpretation of tongues.

You might say that where these attributes or gifts cluster together then there is fruitfulness in our lives and in the work of God in the world. The word cluster evokes another biblical image—that of a bunch of grapes. Here at Ffald y Brenin the biblical character Caleb fascinates us. He and Joshua went against the pessimistic view of their fellow spies and believed by faith that God could give them the land. They recognised the fruitfulness that could be found there and would not be swayed.

> When they reached the Valley of Eshkol, they cut
> off a branch bearing a single cluster of grapes. Two
> of them carried it on a pole between them, along
> with some pomegranates and figs. (Num. 13:23)

Such was the fruitfulness that it took two men to carry it. The cluster of grapes represented the abundance that was there. We believe that where aspects of truth cluster together there is an abundance of life. Jesus came to bring abundant life (John 10:10 NKJV). How do we take hold of that promise?

Here are some truths that have shaped us and give shape to the book you are about to read.

We Are Nurtured by the Compassion of the Father

We live in the world with the compassion of the Father as our foundation. We view the world through His eyes because of His promise:

> The Lord is compassionate and gracious,
>> slow to anger, abounding in love.
> As a father has compassion on his children,
>> so the Lord has compassion on those who fear
>>> him. (Ps. 103:8,13)

We believe that He has crowned us with love and compassion.

We Embrace a Salvation That Touches Every Part of Our Lives

The salvation that Christ bought and brought is not merely for our souls; it is for every aspect of our existence. It heals the body, renews the mind and binds up the brokenhearted. We believe the promise that Jesus spoke:

> The Spirit of the Lord is on me,
>> because he has anointed me
>> to proclaim good news to the poor.
> He has sent me to proclaim freedom for the prisoners
>> and recovery of sight for the blind,

to set the oppressed free,
>   to proclaim the year of the Lord's favour.
>   (Luke 4:18-19)

We believe that He is present to us now, with the power to heal, wisdom for our circumstance and with outrageous grace for our forgiveness.

We Desire Instructed Hearts and Minds

Being a person of blessing requires more from us than words spoken. God calls us to lives of blessing. Values-based discipleship nurtures every part of our being so that being a blessing can become who we are. The prophet and the psalmist hold out a promise to us.

>   Direct me in the path of your commands,
>   for there I find delight. (Ps. 119:35)

>   The Sovereign Lord has given me a well-instructed
>   tongue,
>   to know the word that sustains the weary.
>   He wakens me morning by morning,
>   wakens my ear to listen like one being
>   instructed. (Isa. 50:4)

We seek rhythms of life that will nurture truth within us.

We Want to Be Carriers of His Presence

When we *stand* in His presence, reminding ourselves of His character and His intent, He releases the Spirit to work afresh and anew in our lives, through our actions and in the places we inhabit it, so that we might be *carriers* of the Presence of God. We then *proclaim* the blessings of His presence. We stand on these promises:

> Come near to God and he will come near to you. (James 4:8)

> Again Jesus said, 'Peace be with you! As the Father has sent me, I am sending you'. (John 20:21)

> Heal those there who are ill and tell them, 'The kingdom of God has come near to you'. (Luke 10:9)

We long for the manifest presence of God.

We Are Forerunners of the Blessing of God

We are empowered to declare the will of God for people, places and land. We are His envoys. We deliver the message on His behalf. We take hold of these commissions from God and the promises they contain:

The Lord said to Moses, 'Tell Aaron and his sons, "This is how you are to bless the Israelites. Say to them:

'The Lord bless you
    and keep you;
the Lord make his face shine on you
    and be gracious to you;
the Lord turn his face toward you
    and give you peace'.

    "So they will put my name on the Israelites, and I will bless them."' (Num. 6:22-27)

When you enter a house, first say, 'Peace to this house'. (Luke 10:5)

Mercy, peace and love be yours in abundance. (Jude 1:2)

We want to be those whose words nourish many.

We Seek to Imitate Jesus

All of us who have given our lives to Christ are mandated to imitate Christ (1 Cor. 11:1). As we reflect on His life we are provoked to believe His promise:

Very truly I tell you, whoever believes in me will do
the works I have been doing, and they will do even
greater things than these, because I am going to the
Father. (John 14:12)

We believe greater things are yet to come.

We Believe That Blessing for Others, and Us, Is Nurtured by Community

Love is more than a word. Love is an action. Love is nurtured in us in
our 'impossible communities', our imperfect churches. These healed
and healing people can bring healing to all aspects of the life of the
wider community around them.

We ask God to send His promised Holy Spirit that we might:

Make every effort to do what leads to peace and to
mutual edification. (Rom. 14:19)

Seek the peace and prosperity of the city to which I
have carried you into exile. Pray to the Lord for it,
because if it prospers, you too will prosper. (Jer. 29:7)

We want to be known as a people that have God with us.
The Way of Blessing awaits …

Chapter 1

HERE IS LOVE VAST AS THE OCEAN

He glanced nervously in his mirror, worried that his friend might die at any moment. He had agreed to take her to a prayer meeting. This type of meeting was not something he was familiar with and he was concerned, and had been told by her doctors, that she might die on the way. But his quick glances in the strategically angled mirror suggested that she was coping well with the journey.

In fact she was coping much better than anybody could have imagined. He found the car park beside the church in the valley below the Ffald y Brenin Retreat Centre. When he parked the car he went round to lift her out but she informed him that she was going to walk in. He was taken aback but she instructed him to let her hold onto him. She came in saying to herself, *I got here; God is going to meet me.*

I knew nothing of this.

Suddenly I sensed the breath of God. We were singing the first song of our worship time at the monthly prayer day. We paused and I shared what I believed God was putting on my heart:

> 'You've come here today and it's your very last hope. There will be nowhere else to turn—there is no hope anywhere else. You have come absolutely desperate. You believe that during Prayer Day you will have an encounter with God, which is going to fundamentally change your life. This is what God says: it's not going to happen.
>
> 'That's because He's already met with you on the way here, and if you will just stop now and say 'thank you', you will receive the fullness of what God is giving you. If that's you, I suggest that you stand where you are and say thank you, Lord, and by faith receive what He gives. As for the rest of us, we'll carry on with our worship'.

When we broke for lunch, a lady came to speak to me. She was almost running down the central aisle to the front. 'I want you to know that I'm sure I'm the person that you had that word for', she said. 'Well, that's wonderful', I responded. 'Did you say, "thank you"'?

'Yes I did', she said. I asked if she received by faith what God wanted to give her. She said she believed that she had. I blessed her in Jesus' name to walk in the fullness of it. I asked to be excused and went off to get my lunch.

A few days later the phone started to ring. Church leaders and pastors from Cardiff wanted to know about the amazing miracle that had happened at our Prayer Day. Well, we pray for many people on Prayer Day, and I wasn't aware that there had been anything particularly outstanding on that day.

I asked them to tell me what they had been hearing. I was put in touch with one of our friends who also knew the lady that was at the heart of the miracle story. I called our friend and I began to unravel the astonishing story that lay behind the healing they were referring to.

Chrissie had been ill with ME for many years. She had multiple health challenges and was being rushed to a high dependency unit at her local hospital several times a year to help keep her going and deal with urgent health issues.

She had a friend, Ken, who throughout her illness had been supportive and practical. Occasionally she would want to venture out but one of those car trips came to an abrupt end as she became ill on the way. The paramedics had to actually resuscitate her at the side of the road.

When she asked her friend to take her to Ffald y Brenin she was nearing the end of her life—she had moved into organ failure. It was a serious situation.

In the midst of this someone gave her a copy of *The Grace Outpouring*—the story of how the presence of God was touching many lives at our isolated Retreat Centre in Pembrokeshire. She read it and as she did so, her faith was stirred. She began to believe that if she could visit Ffald y Brenin God would meet her there and would heal her.

She was very clear in her own mind. It was not about the team at the Centre and how effective their prayer might be. She believed that God Himself would meet her there. She asked Ken to take time off work and help her get to our remote valley. He remonstrated with her, 'You know you can't even get out of the bed to go to the bathroom—you can't go anywhere. You're near the end'.

She did not actually know where exactly the Centre was but implored him to grant her this one last wish. He looked us up on the web and was horrified to discover we were 100 miles away, half of which was cross-country on single-track lanes! She insisted that she wanted to go.

He remained deeply wary and called her doctors and shared with them what she was proposing. They were of the opinion that she would die during the journey. They were also of the opinion she would die very soon anyway. They hinted that granting her desire to visit might be better for her, and wished him good luck with his choice! Having looked us up on the Internet and discovered that a Prayer Day was scheduled, he finally agreed to take her as long as she had slept the night before.

When he arrived in the morning he asked whether she'd slept. She said no and he said he couldn't take her. She insisted and he decided that he would take her anyway. He carried her out and settled her in the car. He began to weep. He felt sure that this would be the last time that he would see her alive—she was going to die in his car.

He got into the car and adjusted the mirror so he could see when she passed away. He could then turn round and go to the hospital. He set off on the two-and-a-half-hour journey. What he couldn't understand when he looked in the mirror was that the further he went and the closer he got to Ffald y Brenin, the better she was looking.

Once they arrived, to his complete shock she said she would walk into the hall where we were meeting that day. She heard the words God had prompted me to share as she came through the door. Her heartfelt response was yes and she felt immediately strengthened. So much so that she almost ran the length of the hall to me to say it was her that God had spoken to. I didn't know her at all and there were no clues that a physical miracle was underway unless you knew how very ill she had been. At the close of Prayer Day, Ken drove her up to Ffald y Brenin where they had good fellowship.

The next morning Ken went to see her. He rang the bell and went in as he had a key. He called her name but there was no reply. He looked in the kitchen but there was no sign of anything or anybody. He went to her bedroom door and knocked on it and called her name. There was no reply. He knocked three times and said, 'Unless you call out, I'm going to open the door'. There was no answer, so he opened the door, really nervous about what he might find. There was no one there.

He was really worried now, because he thought she had died in the night and the body had been removed. He was really upset. Suddenly the front door opened and she walked in. There was a mixture of relief and anger. 'What are you doing and where have you been'? he demanded to know. She told him she'd been for a walk by the river. He was incredulous. 'You can't walk; you're not *able* to walk'!

'Ken, God met me yesterday and He healed me. Do you remember'? she gently replied. The day-to-day reality of what had happened to his friend began to really dawn for Ken in the coming weeks. He went to an Alpha course and had an experience with the Holy Spirit. His life changed. They eventually married and now they're involved in a marvelous healing ministry in Cardiff.

This ripple effect of the work of God in bringing heaven to earth is seen in responses to the story of what God did in the health turn-around that Chrissie experienced. Months later, I was travelling and speaking and I shared the story of what God did with Chrissie. A vicar in the congregation burst into tears and couldn't stop weeping. He was a little disconcerted but it awoke an interest in him about the presence of God and the work of the Spirit. He found it very difficult to accept the story as being really true.

He decided to attend one of our prayer days. Many months later he came, but he had never driven on the sort of roads that we have, so he was late and a bit lost. A car overtook him as he pulled in and stopped to ask for directions. A helpful local informed him he wasn't as lost as he thought and that the Prayer Day venue was only about 100 yards away.

He carried on and parked the car. The car that he'd seen go by was also parked there and he parked next to it. As he got out a young woman greeted him and asked, 'Do you come here every month'? She discovered it was his first time ever. She asked what had brought him here, and he explained that he'd heard the story of the lady who had been healed on the way to a monthly Prayer Day. He was honest and said he couldn't understand it, but he knew that he had to come. She said, 'My name is Chrissie, and I'm the person'.

That man had a great encounter with God that day.

But the bigger story of what was happening in our midst started in 1999. The roots of it go back further but it concerns a place that had been set aside as a place of creativity and spiritual retreat. Those who have read *The Grace Outpouring* will know that Daphne and I arrived at Ffald y Brenin knowing that God had spoken to us and to others in highly specific terms about us being there. We were reluctant recruits nevertheless and my reluctance was growing by the month.

For those reading *The Way of Blessing* without having encountered *The Grace Outpouring* story let me give you the gist of what God did. During an anguished time of prayer God told me to stop worrying about how I could do evangelism in a remote corner of Pembrokeshire where almost everyone who visited was already a Christian. He was going to send people to us.

Within hours two people turned up at the door asking about the Centre and were full of curiosity. After a cup of tea I showed them around and when we reached our small chapel I asked if I could speak a blessing (in the next chapter you'll discover why I had been challenged to start blessing people in this way). They agreed and a work of the Holy Spirit began in their lives in the tiny white chapel.

The encounter with God that Chrissie experienced was the experience of many. Buddhist seekers, atheist doubters and blasphemous jokers would find themselves swept into new life by the presence of God. Sometimes our job was to explain and affirm what God was doing in their lives. Other times we helped Christians discover the riches of their own faith and the empowerment that God had for them.

We were on a journey that was part discovery, part trust—when what God was prompting didn't seem to make sense to our human reason. We fretted when there were lulls in the wave of miracles until God spoke to us through an overseas visitor with a message about ebbs and flows. We started to ask what houses of prayer might look like dotted across the nations, around the UK, and around the Mediterranean. We explored what wisdom we could find from the ancient Celtic believers whose insights had shaped our locality and whose prayer warriors were thought to have interceded on the hill above the Retreat Centre.

We started to pray in the chapel four times a day, mixing the beauty of liturgy with spontaneous prayer. One night over thirty people dreamt different dreams and saw different visions that brought the comfort of God to their personal circumstances.

We trusted God when He told me to build a cross on a high point of the land. It seemed impossible to find a stable base given the nature of the rocky ground. But there was a place, a nook where the base could go. It became a place of encounter for many and a thing of great curiosity for the local pagans, one of whom told me that their occult power was diminished after it became part of our witness to the work of God through Jesus.

In the midst of it all, during our journey of discovery, God stretched us. I want to tell you the story of how we discovered more about the role of the believer in blessing others and declaring the desires of God for localities and communities. Blessing others provokes an other-directed heart within us and cannot help but ignite our curiosity about mission and the work of the Spirit. It takes you deep into the idea of the kingdom of God that Jesus constantly spoke of.

You'll discover that the Way of Blessing is not a technique but a way of understanding the person and work of Jesus in bringing a revelation of the Father's heart and the Spirit's work. It renews the patterns of our thinking about mission, discipleship and creation.

So if you're reading *The Way of Blessing* with no previous knowledge of how God has moved among us, then we invite you to discover what God has been doing among us in recent years. If you've read *The Grace Outpouring* join us as we discover more of the grace of God at work in the world and deepen our understanding of mission, the kingdom of God and our role as carriers of and proclaimers of the presence of God.

And if the presence of God is manifest among us we should be ready to experience when: the blind receive sight; the lame walk; those who have leprosy are cleansed; the deaf hear; the dead are raised; and the good news is proclaimed to the poor (see Luke 7:22).

Would this unfold in our lives at Ffald y Brenin? It began to in fresh and new ways.

The Deaf Hear

Two guests were staying who were particular friends of Daphne. On their final day we had invited them to come and have a coffee and a few minutes' fellowship with us before they left. One of the guests came over to break the news that he had lost his hearing aids. Daphne sent the housekeepers over to search their room but they couldn't be found. They thought about their activity that morning but it was limited to their room really. Common areas were searched exhaustively as well. It was as if his hearing aids had physically disappeared.

I asked him what the extent of the difficulty was that this loss would cause. He told me he couldn't hear a thing without them. I immediately registered that he was hearing something! He was distressed however—he explained that he couldn't hear the television news without it being on full volume, even when had his hearing aids in. He was concerned that life would become very quiet until he got replacements.

'How long have you had this condition' was my next enquiry. He had been very hard of hearing for seven years. I lowered my voice a little more and noted that Daphne had realised what was happening and was grinning! I asked him something else very quietly which he responded to, and then I whispered to him and he looked at me as if to say, what on earth are you doing whispering? He answered me. We allowed this to go on for a little while before he suddenly realised that he was hearing absolutely perfectly. And he still does to this very day.

The presence of God had touched him with healing.

The Blind See

One night in the meeting room, during our evening prayers the Holy Spirit came in power. Kelly, one of our visitors, fell to her face onto the floor asking why her eyes hurt so much. Sylvia, the wife of the volunteer leading the meeting, reached down and raised her up by the elbow and said, 'Come and stand with me'. She then gently prompted her: 'Kelly, open your eyes'.

Kelly looked and turned and whispered into Sylvia's ear, 'You see that man over there, I love his shirt'! Everybody heard the whisper and the whole room erupted in praise. She turned and was able to recognise her husband, because she had once had partial sight in one eye in earlier years. 'Look at the size of the grin on my husband's face', she joyfully informed the room.

This story is powerful in and of itself, but becomes more poignant as the story behind the story unfolds.

Kelly and Ian are from East Anglia. They had not been Christians for very long—two or three years at the most. They came from broken backgrounds but they were trying to live in a way that reflected the wisdom of God. They had a strong desire to mark their forthcoming wedding anniversary with a special short holiday.

They spoke to their pastor, who suggested (a bit tongue-in-cheek) that if they wanted to go somewhere quiet and isolated with beautiful surroundings, where nothing ever happens, perhaps they should try Ffald y Brenin.

We were fully booked, so they decided to camp locally. When they arrived, after a long journey, they visited Ffald y Brenin briefly and met a few guests who welcomed them and spoke excitedly of the things that God was doing at the Centre.

That really quite astonished them. They knew nothing about this aspect of the place that they had been directed to. One of the guests suggested that they read *The Grace Outpouring*, which described some of the background to what God was doing. Back at the campsite they downloaded the book onto Kelly's phone. Her husband topped up his worship song collection on his phone.

The next morning they came in on their wedding anniversary for Morning Prayers. They had misunderstood the times and arrived exactly as it ended. To their amazement, instead of being mildly disappointed, they were emotionally churned about it—but weren't entirely sure why.

It was a lovely sunny day, so they wandered down to the high cross and lay on the grass nearby. He listened to worship and she listened to *The Grace Outpouring* audio book—she was blind in both eyes. She was simply amazed. Miracle stories in this day and age were new to her.

They went off for Midday Prayers, had lunch and in the afternoon they went back and lay on the grass. He listened to more worship and she listened to the second part of *The Grace Outpouring*. It had been a mundane but peaceful day. Then they went in for Evening Prayers.

Daphne and I were away that day. Normally there would have been a team member taking prayers in that situation, but we had a couple of volunteers who'd been with us for three months, who were setting off back to Canada the next day and this was their last evening. I'd asked them if they would like to take the Evening Prayers and they were thrilled.

There were an awful lot of people packed into the meeting room—the chapel we often use would not have held them all. There's a moment in our Evening Prayers where we say together:

Lord, wherever spiritual, physical or emotional darkness touches me, I trust You to lighten it.

Suddenly, as the people prayed those words, the Holy Spirit fell on the room in power. People were calling out and weeping and bowing down, but Kelly grabbed her eyes, saying, 'My eyes hurt, my eyes hurt, what's going on with my eyes'? She fell on her knees, crying out that her eyes really hurt. Bryn, who was leading, wondered what he'd done! He was really upset but his wife was saying, 'Lord, this is fantastic, what a wonderful way to have our last evening here'.

Kelly received her sight again during that outpouring of the Holy Spirit. When we got back, which was about ten in the evening, there was a message on the answering machine that sounded a little hysterical: 'I've seen it, I've seen it, I've seen it'! I couldn't understand what on earth it was about, but after playing it a number of times I recognised a Canadian accent, and I wondered if it was Sylvia.

I rang Sylvia and Bryn. 'Thank goodness you've rung', was their immediate response. I asked if all was well. It became clear that they were shaken by something that had happened so I told them I was coming straightaway. I charged off really concerned and found them unable to sit down, pacing up and down and unsure what to do with themselves.

They were in a state of wonder. 'We saw it; we saw it. We have seen somebody who was blind receive their sight'! They had asked Kelly whether she and her husband would stay on until the next day so that I could meet them, and I was so grateful for that.

First thing the next morning I was able to interview Kelly and Ian and discovered that as a little child she had lost her sight in one eye and then had fading eyesight in the other. Eight or nine years previous to coming to Ffald y Brenin her sight had gone completely. She had been totally blind.

As I looked at her, her eyes were never still and were looking everywhere, which slightly concerned me. I mentioned this and she explained what was happening. 'I'm going to have to learn to control that and focus, but I can't stop looking at everything. There's colour, light, and shape everywhere'. She was drinking in the beauty outside, the colour of the carpet, the sun shining on the table and highlighting the different grain. She couldn't stop for a moment.

They explained that back at home they had eight young children, two of whom are adopted. Obviously they wanted to get back home to see their children but they didn't seem to be in a hurry at all, and that confused me. So in the end I said, 'Why are you not in a hurry to get home and see your children'?

They mentioned that they would go and see their pastor first and talk to him. That didn't make sense to me, so I asked why. They explained that they were actually frightened of seeing the children, because everything would be so different. Kelly would be seeing her younger children for the first time ever. She'd seen the older children as infants eight years previously, but with limited vision.

But what if she didn't like how they looked? How they dressed? How they ate their food? Their mannerisms and habits? All the things that she had never seen—how would she cope?

I felt that was a really good reality check and helped put a new spotlight on the stories of the New Testament for me, where we tend to consider the stories in the context of the words, instead of the whole social setting and life experience. Take Bartimaeus, for instance. He had also been sighted, but at some time became blind. He asked for the recovery of his sight and Jesus restored him. At first he followed Jesus with the crowd and you can imagine him sharing his story on the way with all who would listen.

At some point he would have gone home. What would his reception have been like? Was everyone as overwhelmed with joy as he was? Might some doubt that he had ever been blind in the first place? May he have been challenged by doubters amongst his friends or even family? What had been their response when he lost his sight? Did they now feel betrayed? He had earned his maintenance by begging.

How was he going to survive now? We don't know how long he had been blind, but how did he recognise his way, his home, his friends and family? By sight or by sound? How easily would he have adjusted to his new situation, and how did the various members of his network adjust to him?

A year later, which is just a few months past from now, Kelly and her husband came back unannounced to visit us again on their wedding anniversary. They wanted to thank God for meeting them at Ffald y Brenin and giving them such a gift that evening in the chapel. Her eyes are steady. It's interesting that she has difficulty with peripheral vision, but her main sight is fine.

I asked about the children. 'They really struggled to believe that I could see. They kept on gathering around me and asking questions about the colour of their eyes or what exactly they were doing around the room'.

There was a joy that filled her as she recounted these stories. It seemed to be contagious as she and Ian had led many young people to Christ during the previous twelve months.

As we reflect on the work that God does we sometimes think on the fact that God uses those who have a high profile in society, but He also often works through nameless and faceless people. This was brought home to us in a story that brings both aspects together.

When Salvation Overtakes You

It was a joint harvest festival in the valley and we were having a roast dinner after the morning service. We were arranged around the room with about eighty-five of us on different tables. A man suddenly walked over from one of the other tables looking very excited.

He looked at Daphne and me and then he looked at the other six people at the table and told us that Ffald y Brenin had been on the Welsh BBC radio programme and television during the week. Did we know about it?

This was news to us. It seemed that it was during the Welsh language equivalent to 'Songs of Praise'—a regular programme format on mainstream TV which features popular hymns and worship songs alongside personal testimonies, and in particular during a radio broadcast.

It seems that the interview was with a salesman who had visited Ffald y Brenin to try and sell us a photocopier as he had heard that we needed to upgrade.

When he arrived he was given a coffee and he proceeded to explain about the photocopiers that he sold and there was some discussion between our team member Sharon (subsequently retired after seven years with us) and him about the copying needs that we had.

Once that was done, he was surprised to be offered a tour of the Centre. He really didn't want to do the tour, but if that's what it took to sell the photocopier he was happy to go along with it.

As usual the tour ended up in the chapel. Sharon invited him to sit down and told him that it was our normal practice to offer to bless people before they leave. He was not that keen on the idea at all but he was a pragmatic man and reasoned that listening to a short prayer was a small price to pay if he made a sale.

With the passage of time the exact words spoken are lost in the mist of memory but because of the way we train the team we know the basic framework that would have been in her mind as she blessed him. For somebody who's not yet a Christian, we would often say something like this, but in our own words:

I bless you in the name of Jesus, and that God may reveal to you everything you need to know to enable you to be fully who you were made to be, and that you receive everything you need to know, so that the fullness of life might be released to you.

Sharon remembers the way he looked as though something impacted him as she blessed. After a few moments she did the usual thing and left him there because he was still quiet. What she didn't know until we started hearing his testimony was that the moment he was blessed by her the Holy Spirit came to him and began to impart a new understanding of God. He stayed there some time and then he left.

He went down the drive, turned right and stopped to look up at Ffald y Brenin on the hillside. It was a very gloomy day with extremely black clouds and low hill fog. Just at that moment a single sunbeam appeared and focused directly on the high cross. He sat there in his car just staring at the high cross that appeared to be illuminated by a shaft of light. As he stared at it he was transfixed and knew at that moment what Jesus had done for him. He understood the transaction and he made a commitment in response.

He went on in the radio interview to describe how his life has been thoroughly changed; how his relationships have changed; his business practices and his attitudes toward people had been transformed. This is the fruit of a changed life—a changed person with a new heart and a new spirit.

Our dinnertime storyteller in the valley told us the name of the man, obviously thinking that we would know him by his name. It didn't mean much to Daphne and me. But a couple of the older men knew straightaway. He is considered a celebrity as a previous captain of the Welsh national rugby squad (the national sport) who had led them through two World Cups. He had forty-one caps between 1991 and 1996 and was a renowned and famous figure in the 1990s. His testimony is making an impact on many people because of his background, his name and his fame.

It took us a while to work out who had been the team member. He did not mention names in his interview but we contacted a recently retired member and asked if she had prayed for a copier salesman. Yes, came the response, why are you asking? We were able to encourage her with the story of what God had done through her faithfulness and that short blessing.

The Lame Walk

Brigid is a lovely Catholic lady from the Republic of Ireland. She had been very ill for some time. She had been in hospital and had a procedure but had contracted an MRSA infection while she was there. She became very ill and was on life support for a considerable amount of time. She began to improve but had a relapse.

Brigid was housebound and bedbound much of the time and needed an oxygen mask. The smallest effort needed hours of sleep to compensate and she could not spend any length of time in the company of others. She was very sensitive to noise and light and there seemed to be no way of improving things. All the typical symptoms of ME were expressed with her.

She became aware of *The Grace Outpouring* through two friends in Bristol and decided to read it. Faith rose within her and that faith, as she explains it, was not in Ffald y Brenin as a healing place. She was very clear that she wanted to meet with Jesus and that visiting the Centre was part of that.

She persuaded her extremely reluctant husband Jimmy that she needed to come to visit us. He was able to get her to the ferry terminal town and to book them both into a hotel for the night so she could rest after the short car journey. Then he put her on the ferry to Fishguard. Her two friends picked her up and brought her seven miles to our remote retreat.

Brigid takes up the story:

When we got to Ffald y Brenin and I had rested I went to see the little stone chapel, which was very close to my bedroom. My first impression was that it was cold and uncomfortable. What could possibly happen here—there was no Blessed Sacrament! I also discovered that Roy, who I was hoping would pray with me, was away that weekend!

Then I remembered the strong sense I had that I needed to come here. I decided God is bigger than the Blessed Sacrament and Roy, and I decided to trust that God would do whatever He brought me here for.

I went to the Friday evening service, which lasted 20 minutes. It was a lovely prayer time but I could barely tolerate the two verses of a song they sang. I felt that my head would explode.

The following morning I awoke at 6:30 a.m. and felt I should go to the chapel. I said to God, 'You must be joking. I'm so tired and sick and it's dark and it might not be safe to be out there on my own. I'll freeze to death if I go out there in this cold'!

So I ignored the prompting and tried to go back to sleep. An hour later I was still awake, still convincing myself that I was safer in bed. But then I started coughing! I couldn't stop and worrying that I might awaken Rosie and Anj, I got up and put on a tracksuit and coat over my pyjamas and a woolly hat and scarf, and went into the nearby chapel. It was close enough that I could walk despite my limited movement.

It was freezing, but I noticed that I stopped coughing as soon as I went in. I couldn't sit but I noticed some cushions on the floor underneath the large crucifix hanging on the wall. I got some more and made a bed of these under the cross and just lay there and said to God, 'Ok, have Your way and do with me whatever You want'.

And that's where I spent most of the day. I just came out to eat and when I needed to rest in bed. On Saturday evening Rosie, Anj and I had our own prayer service. I was amazed that when a song was sung I asked if we could sing another one. I knew my brain sensitivities must have been improving! My two friends looked at me in wonder!

On Sunday morning I was wakened again at 6:30 a.m. This time I put up no resistance and went to my space underneath the cross where again I lay for most of the day. By Sunday evening my brain sensitivities had improved even more and my walking too. My friends and I went into the chapel after our evening meal. We made a few shy attempts at praying. I felt God wanted us to do something. The answer came so clearly: 'Praise God'. So we started praising, praying, and singing.

The power of God manifested powerfully and I went from being freezing to stripping layers off me. We laughed and cried as the Father, Jesus and the Holy Spirit ministered to the three of us. We were there for about two hours that night. I awoke early again next morning and the two ladies were also awake so we got together in one of their bedrooms and worshipped God again. And the Lord was there in power as in the chapel the night before. Even more healing took place.

After the community prayer time later that morning the man who was leading prayed a blessing on all who were leaving that day. Again I felt I was being powerfully touched by God. Before we left I walked down to reception, for the first time. I was asked if I would like a blessing. Of course I said yes. We walked back up to the chapel and two of the team prayed over me that my ME would be completely gone!

When Jimmy picked me up from Rosslare later that afternoon he couldn't get over the change in me. I sat up in the car and chatted for most of the four-hour journey home (and that was after the boat journey). Two days later I was walking for twelve minutes and my brain sensitivities were completely healed. God has continued to heal me physically and emotionally from all I have suffered during my illness. I have my life back again.

The difference between before and after is so astonishing that a portion of the Catholic press picked it up and interviewed her. They came to Ffald y Brenin and contrasted the pictures of her before her visit and the ones they took as part of their report. It's the most extraordinary transformation of a person that you could see. It's a glowing testimony to the goodness of God.

God has been at work among us. But there is always a backstory with God. He had been at work in me and Daphne to plant the seeds that would bring forth a harvest of joy. It involved us understanding the goodness of God afresh and anew and sometimes for the first time.

If as you continue to read you find the insights here helpful turn to the rear of the book for information on the Way of Blessing course that seeks to equip your Christian community to be a people of blessing.

For further information, visit www.ffald-y-brenin.org, or go to Roy's website, www.roygodwin.org, for additional resources, including study material such as The Blessings Course.

Chapter 2

THE REVELATION OF THE FATHER'S LOVE

Some time ago a young woman came up to Daphne and me as we were breaking for lunch during one of our monthly Prayer Days. Looking quietly at Daphne she said that while Daphne was speaking her deaf ear had popped and she could hear. We rejoiced with her, blessed her and left for a sandwich. The following day she was in our Morning Prayers and asked at the close whether she could have a quick word with me.

She explained that she had suffered a severe head trauma which left her deaf in one ear and that she was weak on one side and had difficulty with co-ordination. Suddenly being able to hear again was absolutely wonderful. The following morning she wanted to share again, this time to say that she was finding herself much stronger and that she could control her weak hand, leg and foot far better. Again we rejoiced with her, affirmed and blessed her and blessed the work that God was doing in her.

The following day was a glorious blue-sky day and very warm. At Evening Prayers we were crowded in the prayer room and all rushed out into the courtyard to get some sunshine and fresh air. God was very present and there was quite a hubbub as everyone chatted excitedly. The young woman approached me again and asked to have a word.

The chatter quietly ceased as everyone moved closer and listened in. She explained that she had undergone many operations on her head and skull and that nothing more could be done for her from a medical standpoint. As well as suffering depression she also had an actual, physical depression on her temple where she had been struck.

The surgeon had said that the bone would not grow anymore and she would carry the wound for the rest of her life. I gently commiserated but ignoring my words she carried on. That morning she had awoken with a sense of heat and tingling across her temple. She had never experienced that before and she felt quite disturbed. She had put her hand to her head but—she looked shocked as she said the words—there was no longer any depression there, just solid bone.

At that point the eavesdroppers looked as though they were going to join me in overflowing thankfulness and praise. But her next words stopped us in our tracks. She carried on by saying, 'I can hear again, and I'm hugely improved in strength and coordination. Also, the impossible has happened: the bone has healed across my head. Doesn't matter much though, does it'?

You could have heard a pin drop. Even the birds seemed to have silenced their songs as they listened; the breeze seemed to hold its breath. I felt lost as I asked what she meant. 'Oh', she said, 'because of the much bigger miracle'. Intrigued, lost, aware of everyone looking at me and wanting to know what was going to happen next (and feeling quite confused), I asked what she meant.

She said that God had revealed Himself to her as a caring Father who loved her, affirmed her, and accepted her, showing that He wasn't at all the angry, disappointed judge she had always imagined. In that moment she recognised Him as the Father she had always longed for in her deepest being. I may have shouted for joy but again she ignored my response and said that there was more.

'More than that'? I queried. Yes there was. She explained that when God revealed His true self to her He also revealed who she really was because she suddenly saw herself in the light of His joy. Looking directly at me she said that now she knew that she wasn't who people had always said she was as a member of a rather despised people group.

To God she was lovely and she filled Him with joy. It had nothing to do with her looks, or her performances—just the outpouring of His passionate, undeserved, unearned, accepting love. She had discovered for herself that God is the Father she always longed for. He's truly amazing in every way.

A new chapter was written in her life that day. It would become part of her backstory. We all have a backstory. My fellow writer, Dave, had an ancestor who was named after Lorenzo Dow—whose ministry in the United Kingdom in the early 1800s was to spark moves of the Holy Spirit and eventually provoke prayer meetings 100,000 strong among the Primitive Methodists.

Dave's mother and father were contemporaries of Duncan Campbell who was used by God in the Hebridean Revival in 1947. Dave does not come to the task of helping me tell the story of Ffald y Brenin as a detached writer—he comes with narratives of revival alive in his spiritual imagination.

All of us, as we step into a renewed understanding of what God might do in and through us, will be building new chapters in our backstory and discovering how the truths we had already grasped fit into what God would have us do. The idea of blessing others also has a biblical backstory and it's rooted in the Father heart of God.

Let me share a little of my story as a way of understanding of what has shaped our perception of blessing at Ffald y Brenin. I know that many of you will have trod some of the difficult paths that I encountered and hope that you will find some encouragement as you read on.

Healing for Damaged Emotions

Like the lady you have just heard about I struggled to understand and connect with the idea of the extent of God's Father love for me. As a young man, even while I was conducting a publicly recognised and effective ministry I had been torn inside. Even as I ministered the love of God to others I struggled to believe that He loved me. I stood with others in comfortable faith that the Lord would heal them and answer their prayers but I didn't believe that He would hear my prayers for myself, only for others.

One of my secret dreams was to go to a truly remote area where I could shout loudly enough to God so that He could hear me. It doesn't take a genius to guess that I had grown up with a father who was deaf to his children's heart cries.

My earthly father had some unusual attitudes. (I'm sure my own children might say the same about me.) If a holiday or a trip were planned, he wouldn't tell us until perhaps half an hour before we were to leave. He didn't want us to be excited. But excitement, looking forward, engaging with imagination, sharing dreams and hopes are all supposed to be part of life.

My heavenly Father promises that the Holy Spirit will release prophetic words through His children, both male and female, and that young men will see visions and older men will dream dreams (see Acts 2:17-18; Joel 2:28-29). He engages us and draws out our involvement by prior revelation. 'For the Lord God does nothing without revealing his secret to his servants the prophets' (Amos 3:7).

One of the most painful experiences of childhood revolved around broken promises. My father worked long hours and when he did come home he was too tired to talk or engage with us kids. To have his attention was a rare thing; to have his company was rarer still. I well remember my excitement when he told me that one summer's evening he was going to take me to the playing field to play football. All through the day I trembled with anticipation; my dad was going to play football with me. When he came home I was shaking with excitement. I sat impatiently whilst he ate his evening meal, drank tea and smoked his obligatory after-meal cigarette.

Then he picked up the newspaper and sat in his customary armchair as usual and read. In the end I wept with grief, anger and frustration. My mother took me into another room and tried to console me by saying that Dad was tired. But he had promised! From then on I knew that promises were not worth a lot and ignoring them was a good way of avoiding disappointment.

But my heavenly Father has filled His Word with many promises that are 'Yes'! in Christ Jesus (see 2 Cor. 1:20). I may have to wait for their fulfillment. I might have to wait for a long time. His timing

seems to run from a different timescale than mine. Yet I am not inse-
cure or left in the lurch. What He promises will ultimately be fulfilled.

My father would see how we were enjoying a meal and when we
had finished would ask whether we would like some more. Of course
as children we would shout yes enthusiastically, to be immediately
told that there was no more. Over time and repetition we learned to
expect that disappointment was normal, that what was offered wasn't
really there. My heavenly Father isn't like that. With Him there is
more than plentiful supply.

Those who look to Him will never be disappointed (Isa. 49:23).
There is abundance, as much and so much more than we could ever
need. Therefore we want to show grace and serve those we encounter
with the abundance of favour that the Lord has prepared for them, too.

If, as you read this chapter, you are thinking that I have been
describing the failure of my earthly father, you have missed the point.
It is the contrast, the hope, joy and healing that I want to show. My
father failed in so many ways, but he was fallen flesh, just like you
and I. He certainly wasn't all bad, and there were occasions of great
joy. He couldn't meet my needs or be the father I needed or longed
for any more than I could be whoever he wanted me to be.

My God is the Father I always longed for. He's truly amazing
in every way. Sharing my inner struggle with a valued friend led
me to pray and forgive my earthly father for placing such a distance
between us. Immediately I could sense the Lord's voice more clearly.
There was much more painful ground still to clear, though.

After several years here I had to deal with my father's death, which
apart from the pain of loss, also brought me face to face with my trou-
bled heart and a mighty God who held the cure. He really does heal the

brokenhearted, not only for everyone else, but to my surprise, for me as well. My God is the Father I had always longed for. He is amazing!

I couldn't believe how deep my grief ran because in truth I didn't expect to miss him very much. My father and I did not get on very well. Some might guess that there is an understatement in that last sentence! For decades I had been exploring the ways in which I needed to let go of thought patterns, behaviours and memories rooted in my dad.

I had been disturbed by my last visit to him whilst he was conscious. He was propped up in bed with my mother sitting nearby. When he greeted me he asked me to tell him clearly whether he was in his last days, so I told him clearly that he was. To my amazement he grinned, grasped my mother's hand and said to us both that he had been waiting all his life to go and see Jesus. I was stunned. I asked him if he would like to take Communion and he said yes.

I knew that there was bread and some sort of drink available but what was I to serve it with? At that very moment the doorbell rang and a local minister stood there. Did she have a portable communion set? Yes of course. And so we sat at the bedside with my dying father and celebrated a simple but meaningful communion service together for the first and last time. Most surprising was when he prayed aloud. If I was surprised by that, I felt even more shocked and disturbed when he thanked the Lord that he knew I had forgiven him long ago.

Then he turned to me, grabbed my hand and said, 'You have, haven't you'? Of course I said that I had, but inside I wasn't at all clear that it was really true. Over the years I had processed many hurts and dealt with them, but to say that I had issued blanket forgiveness was a different thought altogether. Was it true or not? They were the last words I was to hear from him before he slipped into a coma.

The passing of the years has a way of healing past damage by distancing us from the event, which can be escapism if we haven't dealt with the issues involved, but it can also allow for a more balanced perspective of the past. That demands honest and challenging appraisal.

When I was going to become a father myself I vowed to myself that I would be the perfect, loving father that I had always wanted my dad to be. It was extremely painful to discover that I couldn't meet my own demands for performance.

I experienced tiredness, strain, exhaustion, business, busyness, ministry demands; time spent travelling and so on, all at the wrong time, and often through mistaken aspirations. I was doing it for my son; I was doing it for my family; I was doing it to provide for the future. I was a perfect man, perfect husband, and perfect father. Oh, but I wasn't any of those things!

I failed in so many ways and disappointed myself as well as everyone else. I lived to prove my worth and value for my father at any cost, knowing that whatever I did, whatever I achieved would never ever be enough to satisfy him. Why couldn't my father have been different? But why couldn't I be different as well?

Now I looked back and recognised that perhaps he too was disappointed in his own lack of ability to be the good and loving father to me that he desired. Was that what lay behind his asking me to assure him that I forgave him? Again, the bare truth is that he was no more capable of being the ideal than I was. Neither he nor I stood any chance at all if measured against the standard of perfect fatherhood. My God is the Father I always longed for. He's truly amazing in every way.

Jesus came to reveal the Father, breaking the religious and Jewish cultural boxes to let Him out. He is Abba, Daddy. The reason was to break the lies and traditions that held people in dark captivity; and also, because the Father desperately wants to be revealed, to be found. All along He has been present in our loneliness and pain.

In times of sin or rebellion He has been the patient, longing Father waiting to run and greet us at the slightest sign of us looking toward Him. He grieves over our blindness, the lies, caricatures and deceits that have distorted our understanding of who He is. We only have to take a step and He is running to grab us, hug us, and weep over us; a Father who has been grieving over our absence and is inconsolable until we return (see Luke 15:20).

As we take hold of the idea that we can and should pronounce blessing for people and communities our passion for others will be provoked by the character of God exhibited in Jesus. Just as God healed me of the wounds of fallen fatherhood may He also heal your heart, mind, and emotions.

False Burdens and Wrong Expectations

With all our good intentions and buoyed up by our knowledge of the Father's love the need to perform still niggles away at us. I am privileged to spend time with many Christian leaders who come as guests to Ffald y Brenin or who I meet when speaking at various leaders' conferences. Very often, they are able to voice their frustration and disappointment with their lives and their ministry. Very often, but not always, they find themselves battling to satisfy the demands of God, of their own concepts of what it means to be a good or successful leader and of the demands and expectations of their congregation.

No wonder they often exhibit insecurity, a sense of inferiority or are heading toward burnout. The choice often appears to be that they disguise their inner torment and carry on as if on a treadmill, one step at a time, becoming acutely depressed on the way, or throwing themselves into manic activity.

It seems to be a common practice that we criticise leaders (often with the sarcastic or barbed rider, 'I hope you will accept this in the spirit in which it's given'). It is so easy to put unrealistic demands and expectations on others, thereby guaranteeing their failure to satisfy. At that moment we might hear Jesus saying those uncomfortable words to us, 'Woe to you, because you load people down with burdens they can hardly carry' (Luke 11:46).

Part of the purpose of *The Way of Blessing* is to release people from false burdens and wrong expectations. That's what Jesus did, what the apostles did, and it's what we do too. Healing comes so quickly. The need to perform in order to be accepted is deeply ingrained in many of us, and can so easily catch us out.

It was a normal-looking Prayer Day. Each first Tuesday of the month we meet to worship, pray, encourage each other, share testimony, share the word and have opportunity for ministry. We don't advertise it, although it appears on our website, and we never know who might join us but there is always a good crowd. We had got into the habit of asking whether anyone had travelled further than thirty miles to be with us.

A thirty-mile radius is seen as being local in this scattered rural area, and sometimes the odd person had travelled maybe forty miles, and we would clap our hands and welcome them. More recently people were sometimes travelling 100 miles to join with us, which seemed amazing. But when I asked how far people had come on this particular morning I was hearing they'd come an impossible one, two, and even three *thousand* miles!

I asked for more information and learned that we had attendees from North America, Europe, Africa, Asia, Australia and New Zealand. I was stunned and wondered what it might mean. My next thought was to cry out to God and ask Him to help me deliver something that was so wonderful that it would justify their time and money in getting to us. I had fallen straight into the trap of performance and expectation that I placed upon myself and it was a heavy burden. We started to worship and contrary to my hopes there was no flow, no sense of life. It was muted, to say the least.

The team was casting anxious looks toward me and I to them. At the lunch break we wondered together what was wrong. We cried out for help and expected that the worship would really flow when we restarted. It didn't. There was worse; I didn't feel that the word I was bringing was equal to the congregation, and I wanted something new and really inspired. It didn't come.

By the time we got to the end all I could think of was escape. I was embarrassed, angry with God, wondering what was going on. Yet the moment we closed, people started rushing forward, wanting to say how thrilled they were with the worship, the like of which they had never known, and how impacted they were by the word, while some of them testified to being healed of hurts and pain as they listened.

I slipped away in considerable confusion and frustration and as soon as I could I got alone with the Lord. I asked Him to show me what was going on and to my surprise He was awaiting me and ready to respond that very moment. I saw a large banqueting table laid out with scores of places prepared and set. Then He explained that I had a choice. If I wanted to determine what the menu should be, the size of portions and so on, I could do so. On the other hand, He knew every person who would be seated there; He knew their needs and capacity and the food and portion that were perfectly suited to each one.

Some could cope with a small cool dish; others were ready for a very large roast meat meal. He could prepare the food and I could be the waiter who carried no weight of responsibility but who simply served what the master chef had prepared. Which role would I prefer? It didn't take a nanosecond to decide. From that moment all thoughts of performance for acceptance were vanquished. I had been set free.

Nowadays I may be speaking to congregations of thousands, but I am relaxed. All I will do is deliver the dish that the Father has prepared. What happens next is up to Him. I am secure in my heavenly Father's love; I am fully known and fully accepted. I have nothing to prove and no approval to win. My Father's verdict—I am His son whom He loves and in whom He is well pleased. It's an outrageous affirmation from an outrageous God.

Provoking Your Spiritual Imagination

One of my earlier memories is of me standing in the pulpit and praying, reading the scriptures and then preaching my eight-year-old heart out in the Baptist church which my parents helped found, while my mother was busy cleaning the building one weekday. Everyone knew that one day I would be a missionary. It's all I dreamt of until I was into my teens. Later we moved to a village where there was only a Methodist church and by the time I was fifteen I could be found on many Sundays cycling many miles to rural Methodist churches to preach.

Later, when I could drive, I joined a church plant for a nearby American airbase. The Pastor, Malcolm Baker, a very direct Welshman, graciously and generously mentored me and some other young men.

When I was twenty they urged me to go to Bible college where I did a Ministerial Training Certificate, plus a one-year specialist course in evangelism and dipped into some serious theological study. On top of that I did research into the revival history of Wales, Ireland and the USA. My backstory, my expectation of what God might do in and through me, was being formed.

As with all students there was a lot of reading to do and I found myself deeply affected by the writings of Dr. Efion Evans, Jonathan Edwards, Charles Finney and the biography of Rev. Thomas Collins who walked in remarkable revival for the whole of his ministry. These and others inspired me to reach out and see more of God's power to save at work than seemed to be the normative experience around me.

It was at this time that I came across a biography of John Sung and this affected me in a more practical way. John Sung had a relatively short ministry during the 1930s. He was a brilliant Chinese academic who went as a young man to North America to obtain a doctorate in physics. His father was a pastor and John had been converted as a child through a breath of revival that reached China at that time in connection with the revival in Wales.

Back again in China John commenced an extremely effective ministry amongst students. He then joined the Bethel Band, lead at that time by Andrew Gih, a missions grouping that was evangelising far and wide.

Eventually John went alone. He was not short of invitations because his academic prowess had made him famous. An evangelical, John nonetheless had some idiosyncratic views of the Bible and of preaching. He could be very theatrical, sometimes balancing on the communion rail as he preached. He was firmly opposed to Western Pentecostalism.

Then God seems to have got hold of John in a new way; he had a totally unexpected personal experience of the Holy Spirit and became a man with a mission and a man on fire. He remained biblically orthodox and now expected God to move in power, confirming the word with signs following. He would preach the gospel, heal the sick, and where necessary set people free from bondages. The time was short; war was stirring in the region.

In the few short years of John's ministry he travelled incessantly, with the sacrificial agreement of his wife and family, within China and to the nations of Southeast Asia. His ministry was so effective that it is said today that anyone in Southeast Asia who is a third-generation Christian would probably have John Sung somewhere in the family story.

As I read the stories I found myself profoundly stirred by the Lord. This is how I wanted to minister, in step with the Holy Spirit. I wanted to see Him confirm the word with signs following in my ministry. I didn't want to be John Sung; I wanted to be Roy Godwin but with John Sung's God in my life.

Shortly after praying in this way I too was radically changed through an unexpected encounter with the Holy Spirit who turned my life upside down. Immediately I began to see exceptional fruit. I would pray for sick people and in the main they would be healed;

hundreds responded to the gospel invitation, particularly young people. It was a very heady time.

Totally unexpectedly, nowadays I sometimes find myself travelling and preaching in John Sung's footsteps. Whilst in Southeast Asia a few months ago I was chatting with a pastor who told me that he was a third-generation Christian. Apparently his grandmother had been a terror to Christians, actually chasing them out of the house if they dared come near. She was blind and a vehement hater of Christianity.

Some friends persuaded her to go with them to a John Sung meeting attended by thousands. When he walked into the packed church he went straight across to her, laid hands on her and she received her sight immediately and gave her life to the Lord. Now her grandson, a third-generation Christian, is leading others to the Lord.

In a few short years it is estimated that 100,000 people surrendered to the Lord through John Sung's missions. I was thrilled to be taken to the church where John Sung had preached to thousands when he went to Singapore, see the simplicity of his boarding room, and stand behind his travelling pulpit.

Could We Be a People of Blessing?

As I grew older other writers, thinkers, and friends would fan into flame the sparks lit in my life by John Sung. I have written about my earlier years at Ffald y Brenin in *The Grace Outpouring*, and described there my growing understanding of early indigenous Christian practice amongst the Celtic nations. The idea of 'Colonies of Heaven', a term used by a Celtic saint, inspired Ian Bradley to name a book after it, and it began to change my understanding of basic principles of developing Christian community.

The attributes of Colonies of Heaven include: An understanding that all are welcome; of prayer being at the heart; a simplicity of life; a welcoming hospitality; a healing place; a people who are quick to forgive; an admonition not to take offence; a place where mercy always triumphs over judgment; and leaders who don't climb up the ladder but who dig down deeper that they might be the servant of all.

They knew all about blessing. One of the Celtic saints was the godly Columba who lived in the seventh-century on Lindisfarne, Holy Island, from where he exercised an amazing ministry. The story is told how, one day, he was in wild country between Hexham and Carlisle in a time of plague, preaching and confirming the newly baptised when a group of women appeared on the edge of the forest, carrying a young man who was wasting away with a serious illness.

Putting the young man down, they approached Columba and asked whether he would bless the young man. He looked at him and saw that he was in a desperate plight. He withdrew to pray for some time, then turned to the young man and blessed him. His condition instantly changed; within an hour he was eating and talking and left on foot with those who had brought him.

We increasingly see people manifesting healing in response to a word of blessing, as well as through personal ministry. A brief time ago I was enjoying time with the team and rehearsing some of our story and our values. Over a number of years some team members will move away or retire, to be replaced by others. The Team itself is also growing in size. For some of them, sitting together in the farmhouse, a lot of this was new and they were excited. How could they learn more?

These historical Celtic Christian communities were mission shaped in the context of a saving God and a kingdom to come which was breaking in on earth already. They were what I longed to see. Little did I know how effective mission was about to break forth in a torrent to the nations from our little Centre.

The Father's Joy

When we reluctantly accepted the call to serve at Ffald y Brenin, I was confused as to why we should have been called here. My life had pretty well imploded and I was seeking to make sense of the mess. The Trustees were well aware of the situation and examined it carefully. In prayer the Lord confirmed that they were to invite us unanimously, not knowing that I had agreed with Daphne that anything less should stop us proceeding.

Later, as I called to the Lord He revealed that He wanted to create a House of Prayer at Ffald y Brenin. Whilst overjoyed, I couldn't see how that could happen in a remote location with no Christian population to draw from. Yet here we are now, with over 10,000 people a year from around the world coming to seek the Lord, attend mini conferences, while streams of mission are pouring out to nations, team members are travelling, there are wonderful stories of people encountering the Lord, sometimes for the first time, healings, deliverance, and so on.

When Jesus was baptised in the Jordan by John the Baptist the Father couldn't hold back His joy. Breaking through the realm of eternity into our world of time and space He thundered forth with, 'This is my Son, whom I love; with him I am well pleased' (Matt. 3:17).

Mark remembers it as being slightly more personalised: 'You are my Son, whom I love; with you I am well pleased' (Mark 1:11). The NLT says, 'You are my dearly loved Son, and you bring me great joy'. What a statement. What affection. What joy; what affirmation. As a youngster and even as a young man I had longed to feel loved, affirmed. There was a gaping hole in my heart, in my emotions, and it never got easier. For years I had battled against suicidal desires.

'You are my Son', speaks the Father to Jesus in front of the crowds. A public affirmation with fatherly delight—that's settled then. What acknowledgement before men; what security! But well pleased, joyful? Jesus hadn't done anything yet; His ministry hadn't begun. The approval was totally disconnected from His performance. And when His ministry did commence He had nothing to prove because He had already been totally accepted, acknowledged and approved before He started. This was important; He obeyed the Father's will and purpose out of a love relationship, not out of a desire to win His Father's love by performing well. In stark contrast, I felt so unloved and unlovable that I found myself trapped in a permanent desire to perform desperately well in every way so that someone somewhere might approve of me.

As I looked at those verses I remembered that I too am a child of God. My heavenly Father has personally chosen me and He's not disappointed, even when I disappoint myself and everyone else. How can that be? He is love, mercy and grace wrapped up in endless support and patience toward me. He knows how frail I am, how weak, yet He endlessly takes me as I am. Instead of nasty retorts when I stumble or fail to meet some real or imagined demand, He is there to speedily help me up, dust me down and assist me to start again.

Merciful, merciful, merciful is my Father. He is the only One who can meet my deepest needs, and, most amazingly, longs to do so. When I don't want to look in the mirror, He gazes at my face with such overwhelming compassion and still more acceptance, clothed in joy. When others speak ill of me He speaks well of me. When the enemy attacks, He helps me to stand. Such grace—He is not ashamed to be known as my Father, to own me as His child.

Jesus says that if we are weary and heavy laden we can come to Him for rest. His yoke is easy and His burden is light. I wondered about the weights that I carried in contrast to those words and realised that they were a big, mixed bundle. There were my insecurities, the weight of things not said by my father, as well as many that were said. There were all the demands of trying to present myself as a whole person when I was so broken inside. Then there were the weights of expectation always crushing me.

Some were unachievable, such as those of my father, but then there were the demands of my Heavenly Father, of Christian leaders, of 'churchianity's' religious culture. There were the condemnations of my own heart as well as of the enemy. As for my sins, my failures … What about my disappointments, and the knowledge that I so easily disappointed others around me as well as those dearest to me?

Come to me and find rest. (Matt. 11:28)

Then I sensed the Father's outrageous love and acceptance of me, even of me, made by grace a child of God. My performance was not the measuring rod of my life; the price He was willing to pay that He might have me *long before I could have pleased Him or sought to influence*

Him has become the standard. The cross is His personal affirmation of me personally, of my value to Him, of my worth. On Calvary's hill He publicly owned, loved and valued me. This is how we know what love is (1 John 3:16). There is therefore no more condemnation; no, neither is there a demand for performance to win love (Rom. 8:1).

To see people's physical ears or eyes opened through the mighty name of Jesus is a wondrous thing and we rejoice with great joy when we see it. What happens with greater frequency at the Centre is that God breaks through into someone's understanding of who He is and there is an immediate change of relationship. Sometimes this has happened through the sharing of the word, but very often it has been through sovereign revelation.

I have found myself growing in the experiences I had always longed for. Not only did I know the truth but I was walking in it, which is when it sets you free (John 8:32). A wonderful retired bishop friend of ours expressed it so clearly; this is how the kingdom works. You know you are loved and you find yourself loving others.

You know you are forgiven and you find yourself forgiving others. You find yourself accepted and of course you find yourself accepting others. There is an outflow, a reflection of what He has done for you, toward others as your heart attitudes change. And of course, aware of such undeserved blessing you want to share more about the kingdom of God—the idea about the heart of God that blessing expresses.

For further information, visit www.ffald-y-brenin.org, or go to Roy's website, www.roygodwin.org, for additional resources, including study material such as The Blessings Course.

Chapter 3

A KINGDOM OF BLESSING

'Ruth' (not her real name) had been at Ffald y Brenin for a few days. It was clear that she had severe difficulties that she was carrying and living with. Daphne, with her big soft heart and to the shock of the rest of the team, invited her to the conference we had planned for that weekend despite the fact that we actually had a long waiting list.

The meetings were full and Ruth had to sit near the front, despite her preference for being at the back. The worship was wonderful but I prayed with the worship leader in the afternoon and together we asked the Lord for more of His presence for the evening. He answered, and that night the church was ringing with praise and the sound of musical worship. The presence of God felt tangible.

Suddenly I noticed the lady who we're talking about, standing near the front with her head forward. Her face was purple, her eyes looked as though they were going to burst out of her face and her tongue was distended. Russ Parker, one of the speakers that weekend, had already noticed and went straight to her.

I saw him touch her neck and speak a word and then turn around and come back to the speaker's area. I saw her instantly relax and then a little bit later I noticed her with her hands in the air, her face uplifted and absolutely lost in praise and worship.

At the end of the evening she came up to me to share her story. When she was eighteen she decided that she wanted to be a worshiper of God (those were her words). She found a local church and remains there decades later.

She would sit at the back because she has suffered with depression. Hospitalisation and medication had done little to help and she remained visibly miserable. She wanted to be there to honour God, but didn't want to be off-putting to anyone else. If she tried to open her mouth and sing, she immediately had a sensation of being physically choked and she couldn't breathe. She thought she was going to die. So she didn't sing.

Earlier that evening she had felt caught up in the worship but the moment she did, she felt she was being strangled. Russ spoke very clearly when he went across to her: 'In the name of Jesus, I release you from what is choking you'. Immediately she could breathe and was free and was able to worship as never before.

The next morning I invited her to share what had happened the previous night during the thanksgiving service at the close of the conference. That seemed safe, but there's a principle in those situations that I forgot. Don't ask people questions when you don't know what the answers are going to be!

Were things different for her, I enquired? 'Oh yes', she responded. 'My heart is light and I can smile, and I can sing for the first time'. Cheers resounded around the hall. I ventured that she must have slept well. 'No—I couldn't sleep last night for weeping about the pain'. She began to sob and said that God had revealed to her the root of the choking sensation. It was buried deep in her memory.

She remembered it being close to her fourth birthday in the garage of her father's home. She was frightened. A strange man was very noisily trying to break into the garage. He broke in, rushed across and grabbed her, and removed the noose from around her throat moments before it would have been too late.

She was never to see her father, who had tried to hang her from the rafters, ever again. But her identity was scarred by the rejection implicit in her father's attempt to kill and abandon her. God's intervention the previous evening had reminded her He had never let go of her. The atmosphere was electric as she shared her story and there were many tears amongst the congregation. There was much else to heal in her life but the process had begun.

I shared that story with a vocal specialist some time later. She turned away and appeared to be wiping tears from her eyes. She composed herself and said that her choking issues were consistent with what they knew about responses to trauma. It was wonderful that she had been healed.

But then she asked one of those questions that make you want to wince, cry and get angry all at the same time. 'If it is true, as it seems, that the Jesus you speak of has power to heal, how could this lady be in church for so long and not be set free before now'?

There are no easy answers to that question but across the body of Christ we have not always grasped how the Bible reminds us that salvation and healing are both part of the good news. We have not grasped the full extent of the kingdom message and authority that Jesus proclaimed and now delegates to us.

Is Our Gospel Too Small?

Many of us have read J. B. Phillips and been provoked by *Your God Is Too Small*, his book that challenged us. That was many years ago but the phrase stays with you. In my own life I began to be aware that the good news about Jesus that I was preaching was too small. My version of the gospel had become too small.

We are all prone to reducing life to short sayings. In our mainstream culture people may say some of the following: get what you can while you can; every man for himself; science offers the hope of a new and peaceful future; new hope for a transformed world; equal society through our creed. These ideas come and go, undone by genocide, nuclear bombs, and a horror at a society that cares little for others.

Perhaps we as Christians are also prone to one-sentence gospel summaries. Many of the older hymns focus on heaven. We tell ourselves that Jesus came that we might all go to heaven. Or we opt for: Jesus came to pay the price of sin so that we might all go to heaven.

All of these short sayings carry a massive truth within them. Jesus did open a new and living way into the heart of the Father. He did die for our sins.

But the gospel, the good news that Jesus brought, was a bigger story than that.

> After John was put in prison, Jesus went into
> Galilee, proclaiming the good news of God. 'The
> time has come', he said. 'The kingdom of God has
> come near. Repent and believe the good news'!
> (Mark 1:14-15)

The kingdom of God breaking into our lives is more than a one-time event. Jesus calls us to respond to it by repenting. The root meaning of this word suggests a change of direction. Repenting is much more than sorrow and regret over past rebellion against God. It is a call to live differently because God has broken into time and space through Jesus and introduced the rule and reign of God to our everyday lives and communities for today.

His early followers had to turn around in so many different ways.

- The fishermen became fishers of men
- The tax collector, whose job it was to take, became a giver
- Simon the Zealot, committed to his nation, turned toward the kingdom of glory

The kingdom is near because Jesus is here. He carries and embodies the kingdom. The divine drama was unfolding through His life and a new story was emerging for us who would follow Him. Many of us have grasped the outlines of that story and might tell it like this:

- God created the earth
- God fellowshipped with humanity

- We fell through sin
- Separation, spoiling, and disjointedness was the result
- Jesus came as the Saviour
- He paid the price for our rebellion at the cross
- One day we will be with Him
- Eden will be recreated

This is all wonderfully true but it's still not the fullness of the gospel that Jesus was proclaiming, which is 'the rule of God' expressed in the kingdom of God—His will being done on earth as it is in heaven has come.

Let's look at how Jesus interacted with the people He met, as they encountered Him. How does His welcome provoke us about our welcome? It is quite shocking and can be summarised in two words in most cases. Grace first. Or in five words: Kindness leads us to repentance.

His initial message is: follow Me. (It's not about forgiveness or judgment at this point—which might challenge our patterns of thought about proclaiming the gospel.) It's simply about people coming as they are. The Holy Spirit then opens their understanding as to who Jesus is and what He is like.

- Peter declares: 'You are the Holy One, the Son of God, the Messiah'. Jesus replies: 'Blessed are you; human wisdom didn't bring you to this point. This is divine revelation' (my paraphrase).

- To Nicodemus, the orthodox teacher of law—Jesus reminds him that understanding and being an expert in law and grasping for the righteousness of the law is not enough. Grace has to take hold of him.
- To the woman caught in adultery—Jesus says, 'I do not condemn you. Go, you are free to leave. Don't do it anymore' (see John 8:1–11).

Jesus models the gospel and says:

- To the blind—receive your sight.
- To the paralysed—rise up and walk. (By the way, your sins are forgiven.)
- To the deaf—hear.
- To the feverish—be released.
- To the unclean—you are cleansed.
- To the dead—rise up.
- To the demonised—be set free.
- To the outsider who doesn't belong and has no place—you are welcome.

The spirit of conviction will at some point come upon these people and they will have to deal with the question of sin. That is the job of the Holy Spirit, who has been sent to convict of sin. But we often try and do God's work. We pressure people and sometimes they even give in. Let this thought provoke us: Should our focus in bringing the good news be wider than a focus on sin?

Jesus crosses the religious and social boundaries to engage with outsiders and includes them in—the Samaritan woman at the well was a woman, a follower of another creed and had married often—all things that would have caused concern for the religious people of Jesus' day. He offered her the water of life.

He welcomed the poor—feeding the hungry in thousands. The disciples had a common purse, so they could distribute to the poor as they travelled. The gospel that Jesus proclaimed was not simply a call to make a small verbal transaction with respect to our sin. It was an invitation to see the words and works of Jesus as the essence of what it meant for the kingdom of God to break in.

The gospel was much more than words or creeds. It was the goodness of God in action. It was the compassion and mercy of God, who has seen the mess of our lives and has groaned for us and over us. The kingdom of God coming near through Jesus was an expression of the love of the Father for His children.

God has one intent, to have mercy on us and heal us; to restore us and make us whole. But we don't always grasp that, despite the clear and consistent witness of the scripture. If we're honest many of us wrestle with it. We're hoping He heals but we're not sure.

I just love the way God moves and makes it very clear that the story is about Him and not us. This following story captures the 'I hope He does but I'm not sure' reality.

A Baptist minister that none of us here had ever heard of or come across drove early in the morning across his part of England and the full breadth of Wales, turned up at Ffald y Brenin, exited his car, saw a guest and said, 'Can you point me to the high cross'? They did so and he went there.

He didn't let us know that he was here and we didn't know that he was around or who he was. He apparently spent some length of time crying out to God at the high cross, but he was expecting a response of some sort—that's what he'd come for. As far as he could see, nothing whatsoever happened. There was no sense of breakthrough or touch from God or anything.

In the end he was really saddened and gave up. He didn't come and tell anyone that he was here, but went back to his car and drove home. He was a very disappointed man.

The next morning, he went into the bathroom and took handfuls of water to wash his face. He turned to the towel and realised that his hands were covered in bits of something and he couldn't work out what it was. He went back to the sink to wash his hands and saw that the sink was covered in bits of stuff, which he didn't understand. He looked in the mirror and saw that all of his skin cancer had fallen off and he had beautiful, clear skin.

We quickly learned about it because people from the community where he lived started turning up here very quickly saying, isn't it amazing? We've seen it with our own eyes! We subsequently discovered that for several weeks, local people were knocking on his door and he'd open it and they would just stand and stare at his face and then say they were sorry but that they couldn't remember why they'd called!

The kingdom came for him but not in the way he had expected. The goodness of God came near to him. Our heart response to the goodness of God is an important foundation if we are to embody and declare kingdom blessing.

Worship and the Kingdom of Blessing

As a young teenager I went to a weekend conference held in an extremely snowy and cold Cambridge College. The first item the following morning was simply listed as: QT.

Neither the lad sharing my room nor I had a clue as to what it meant. So, the next morning we got up and roamed around, trying to discover where we were supposed to be going. We had no joy. At breakfast we asked some of the others about the QT but they just laughed, looked sheepish and said nothing.

Finally I tracked down a leader and first heard the phrase—Quiet Time. I was taught that if you were a Christian it was your bounden duty to get up early in the morning and spend some time reading the Bible and praying. I was shocked; no one had ever told me, and apparently God was extremely disappointed in me.

So I had to put it right. The conference organisers pointed me to their daily Bible readings, which apparently were approved by God Himself! That was settled, then. I didn't need to read the Bible. I could just read the notes.

Knowing how to pray for ten minutes was more of a challenge, but again they had the answer; a simple guide to using mnemonics to take you through things like thanksgiving, adoration, praise, petition and intercession. I felt as though I had fallen into an alien culture with alien language.

The one thing that was never mentioned was worship. Why was that?

It is very difficult to worship out of an intellectual assent alone. Religiosity can produce magnificent pageants of worship that are pleasing to the eye or ear without touching the heart at all. Orthodox theology can produce great words that are theologically correct, but they don't necessarily touch our spirit.

For the Christian, real worship flows from a heart relationship that is shaped by passionate, unending love. God supplies that. Worship is our response to such generous grace, such generous goodness. Some of the great times of worship with the team here at Ffald y Brenin are launched by their response to a passage of scripture that has come alive.

At other times, it might be a response to a testimony from one of our guests. Sometimes it is the response to the awesome, if not overwhelming, 'felt' presence of the Lord Himself. Notice the repetitive word—response. It is heart business. God has spoken, acted or revealed something. Worship is response; it comes out of genuine relationship.

At other times, particularly publicly, the very beginning of worship can seem to release the presence, leading to yet greater worship. At one of our monthly Prayer Days we began to sing and then stopped, with many falling to their knees before the King of Kings. On another occasion we were ministering in a large church in a large English city. As soon as our musicians led the first line of the first song there was such an outbreak of the Lord's presence that there were people on the floor crying out to Him.

At the end of the event the pastor explained to us that there had been previously a major breakdown of relationship between the leaders to the point that he was about to resign. When the presence of the Lord rushed in, they were reconciled in tears, brokenness, and forgiveness. The kingdom had broken in.

For some reason worship has become equated with music to the extent that if someone says they are going to worship we imagine that they mean they are going to sing. But worship is not music alone; all forms of activity can be worship. Simply thanking God and telling Him He is good is acceptable. There may be a painting, a landscape (or seascape), a story or a poem that triggers a move within our hearts to worship Him.

Essentially, to worship Him is to give Him His worth. Well, He is glorious, perfect in holiness, magnificent, wonderful. How can we give Him His worth? What do we have that can possibly be a worthy offering? The answer of course is that true worship takes place when we offer our whole selves to Him as a living sacrifice; that is what He sees as holy and acceptable.

In our daily Rhythm of Prayer at Ffald y Brenin we have worship, Bible reading and prayer in some balance. This reflects our personal lives and the balance we seek to maintain in private. Originally written to help us worship in our chapel times, thousands of copies are now in use around the world in many languages.

Can liturgy help us worship? Isn't it in opposition to the freedom and inspiration of the Holy Spirit? For us there are times when we don't use it at all; times when we lay it down part way through; times when we are deeply moved to worship because the words have caught the breath of the Spirit. It can be a wonderful way of priming ourselves for worship and prayer so at the end we might simply carry on in the Spirit.

Worship can immerse us in the character of the One who blessed us with salvation. It instructs our tongues that we might say the words that sustain the weary. It prepares us to be a people of blessing. It prepares us for the task of blessing others.

Kingdom Come: The Prayers of the Kingdom

Prayer and worship are at the core of who we are and what we do at Ffald y Brenin. If what we do is not grounded and rooted in prayer, it might be good; it might last for a while; but in the longer term it will wear us out and will not stand.

Of course, what we are when we come together has to be rooted in our character and prayer life in our personal, unseen lives. That poses a challenge for us because we can pretend in public. In real life there are times when we are not doing so well with our personal prayer times yet we still have those more public times where we present an 'all is well' face, but if we fail to sort out our personal walk by ignoring it for a sustained period of time we run into trouble. The biblical word for that pretence is 'hypocrite', referring to the actors who held a mask in front of their real faces.

For us, when we pray we find worship arising. When we worship, prayer bursts forth. They are like God-honouring twins. We find there are times when all we want to do is worship, and at other times we seem to be immersed in prayer at every moment. These are 'times and seasons' in our experience.

Whenever I am invited to speak on prayer I explain that I see myself as a practitioner but lay no claim to being an expert. We are all learners on The Way. It seems to me that the point is not fundamentally whether we pray, but rather, are we praying as Jesus taught us to pray?

For some reason the Our Father is termed the Lord's Prayer, as though it is the only prayer of Jesus that is recorded. In common with countless others, when I was a child my mother patiently taught it to me by rote and I grew up expected to recite it each bedtime and at church services.

The key word here is 'recite'. It taught me to meet others' expectations and enabled me to participate on a Sunday, if only for a minute. What it didn't do was teach me about prayer. I find compassion welling up within me when I encounter so many Christians who have recited/prayed the Lord's Prayer for years, maybe for decades, but have never entered into real prayer.

When the disciples, orthodox and experienced believers in God, saw the prayer life of Jesus they realised what a sizeable gap there was between their experience and that of Jesus. 'Lord, teach us to pray'—take us beyond the daily prayers at the synagogue; help us understand Your heart.

I imagine that Jesus had been waiting for that question for a while. His response was not that they should recite a piece of liturgy every evening in private and then collectively on the Sabbath. Rather, He used a common rabbinic teaching method of the time and gave them a skeleton, a framework, upon which they could put flesh. He didn't say—these are the words to say. Rather, He said—this then is how you should pray. I'm not suggesting for a moment that there is anything wrong in praying the Lord's Prayer as it is, in private or corporately.

As we enter into the depth of the framework and explore it, our simple recitation becomes so much more meaningful to us:

Our.

I come as a member of a new family, a royal priesthood, and a holy nation. I am not alone.

Father.

Archbishop Rowan Williams wrote, 'This is not an academic word coolly spoken. It is the voice of a dependent child awakening from a terrifying nightmare'. It is a word of inclusion into a family, a warm domestic word not used of God until Jesus reframed the relationship. It is an invocation of His manifest presence in our daily realities.

In heaven.

The place of authority, and I can come boldly straight into the heart of it and stand in the most secret councils.

Hallowed be Thy name.

Come and be God with all Your attributes and character, fully manifest, in my life, family, community, college, workplace, etcetera, so that people are overwhelmed by Your love, goodness and mercy. Essentially we are crying out that God might break out as God so that the result is our neighbours hallowing His name, not as a duty but as an expression of awe, wonder and love.

Your kingdom come, Your will be done on earth as in heaven.

The heart of the outline: Invoking the coming in of the kingdom, the rule of God, plundering Satan, binding his works, and setting prisoners free. Heaven is coming to earth now.

Give us today our daily bread.

Jesus was not referring to anything other than dependency on God for the basic supply of bread. As with the Old Testament manna, bread was a basic necessity of life at the time.

And forgive us our trespasses.

Offensive to the religious across the millennia who would expect this heading to come well before physical supply of bread because bread isn't spiritual in their view.

As we forgive those who trespass against us.

This is the reminder that the flow of forgiveness is linked to our forgiving of others, otherwise we are like the unjust steward who ended up in disgrace. This is an echo of the key biblical motif that we forgive because we are forgiven.

And lead us not into temptation.

The Holy Spirit took Jesus into the wilderness to be shaped through His testing by the evil one. I want to learn from His example and keep my ears open to the Lord. Don't let me come to the point where the only way He can grab my attention is through the battles of temptation.

But deliver us from (the) evil (one).

We need to trust in His delivering power even while we put on our armour of protection.

For Thine is the kingdom, the power and the glory.

He has the power to deliver the goods. He is faithful to His word and powerful to keep it. These subversive prayer words refute the claim to divinity of the Caesars in Rome. They are the words of the rebel Jesus, the true King, establishing a new kingdom.

This kingdom creed establishes a new relationship with God, asks Him to act to cause His name to represent the holiness of God in action in the world, asks again for a foretaste of heaven on earth and hints at justice in its request for daily bread. It asks God to forgive us and cause us to forgive. It seeks assistance though the hard times and temptations and refuses the claims of a pagan imperial power.

How can we voice these words and not burst into worship? Worship and prayer will gladden the heart of God—but they will also shape us into carriers of blessing, bringing more than words.

Bringing Life

It isn't simply that God has come along as a supplier for people's needs. That is a pagan mind-set. As the Lord's Prayer shows us, He had come to bring life. To the Gadarene demoniac He said, 'I deliver you so you can live again'.

Jesus came to show us the Father—to reveal God to us. When we want to know what God is like we look at Jesus. The book of Hebrews tells us that Jesus is the exact representation of His being, not a sketch or a fleeting glimpse.

> The Son is the radiance of God's glory and the exact representation of his being, sustaining all things by his powerful word. (Heb. 1:3)

When we see what Jesus does, we see what the Father is doing—because He only does what He sees the Father doing (John 5:19). He embodies the Father's compassion; He speaks the Father's words.

Like the suggestion made by Naaman's maid that he bathe in the river to receive his healing, they are not always easy to undertake or obey. They can sometimes feel like foolishness.

On the farmhouse lawn at Ffald y Brenin there's a waterfall. It's always lovely, but in the winter it can become quite beautiful when the ice forms around the edges and where the water splashes on the rocks. Many people have taken glorious photos of the ice, the sunlight and the waterfall.

A young woman was here as a guest. Most people would have deemed her very attractive, but she was suffering from an appalling skin condition. Truly dreadful. I looked at her and sensed God saying that He wanted to heal her. But I had to leave straightaway so I just entrusted her to the Lord and that was that.

One of the first things the team told me on my return was the miracle that had taken place. She came to Ffald y Brenin desperate for God to heal her. She'd heard that God did things like this at the Centre. The disease that she had was untreatable and incurable, so only God alone could be her help.

She didn't tell anybody this when she arrived. Initially she didn't even come to the Rhythm of Prayer, which is voluntary anyway. After a couple of days she started to mix with people and she began to hear people talking about what God had done and how He'd met them while she was there, and that raised her hope and faith.

She didn't tell anyone about her desire to be healed.

Her hope was building, however, and she was trusting God for Friday to be the day of healing, because she was leaving the next morning. That evening she wept.

She awoke really disturbed the following morning and looked at the state of her skin and really shouted at God in her heart. *Why have You not answered my prayers? Why have You allowed me to put my faith in You, but nothing has happened? Why is it that You have clearly met with other people while I've been here, but you won't meet with me? Is it because You're like everybody else? Is it because You see me as worthless and spoilt and ugly? That's what everybody else says. Is that who I am? God, I so much desired You to meet with me.*

And then to her amazement, she was very aware of God saying to her, 'Go and wash in the spring water'.

Now that stunned her. She immediately thought of the waterfall on the lawn and the ice and the fact that it was a bitter time, temperature wise. She struggled and said, 'God, I can't do that'. She was a very reserved young woman and was horrified at the idea of unrobing and stepping into the icy water of the highly public waterfall!

So she asked the Lord for something else to do. He said, 'Go and bathe in the spring water'.

She argued with God for a while but she could not bring herself to do it. She was really upset.

She packed her bags to leave and then thought she would have a quick bath before she went. She had a bath and went home. The next day she got up quite early, still feeling disappointed and heavy. She glanced down at her arm and noticed that she had beautiful, clear skin. She checked her other arm and it was the same. She dashed to the mirror to see that she was totally and completely healed.

This gave her a huge problem because she felt that she'd said no to God. So she waited until 9:00 a.m. because it was a Sunday morning and then she rang Ffald y Brenin. She spoke very rapidly and explained the situation and her own confusion to the team member on the other end of the phone. Gently our team member told her, 'All the water here is spring water. There is no other supply. You had a bath in spring water—you did what God asked you to do'. The pressure was lifted and she was truly able to rejoice.

It was a day of life and restoration for her.

Kingdom Blessing Demonstrated

With that in mind we need to be aware that Jesus came to show us ourselves. He came to show us how it is possible to live in flesh, in human form. With the anointing of the Holy Spirit, full of the Word of God, a new life emerges with a power that is rooted in God. We can be in the world, but not of the world. Jesus came to model ministry. He told us that if we believe we would do greater works (John 14:12). He invites us to step into the kingdom now, and then become carriers of the kingdom to others.

We don't go alone. The book of Joel reminds us that God will pour out His Spirit on all people. It doesn't say merely His followers. It is liberally poured out. It's just that many among the *all people* have not yet realised it or have turned their faces away.

The implication however is that the Holy Spirit is going before, working in lives and circumstances, even when people have not yet come to understand and see it. Dreams and visions may be being planted in hearts.

How does that work out in the nitty-gritty of life?

When we meet the sick, we have the possibility of saying, 'I have good news for you'. Would you like to be set free? I set you free in the name of Jesus. That is the bringing of the gospel—the good news to that person.

When we meet the lonely person, who feels cut off and unwelcome. When we say to them, come in, join us—in itself this brings the kingdom of God near to them.

When we meet the demonised person (don't always be looking for demons, by the way—but when they manifest, you can deal with them). We declare deliverance for the afflicted so that new life can be found.

Jesus commissioned the disciples with this message of the kingdom of God (see Luke 10). Jesus rules with power and authority and He sent His disciples out to do likewise. 'Become friends with the people. Heal the sick' (Luke 10:9). He instructs them to proclaim the good news of the kingdom. 'Even the demons are subject to us', they report upon their return (Luke 10:17).

As you continue to read about our embrace of the Way of Blessing be aware that what is happening around us at Ffald y Brenin is not because we're very holy and we pray good prayers. It isn't because of our performance. Our vision for mission, discipleship and the presence of God among us is rooted in what we believe Jesus tells us and shows us about the emergence of the kingdom of God. This perspective will help make sense of everything you read in this book.

Along the way we'll continue to reflect on calling, knowing God, the place of revelation, intimacy with God, the equipping of the Holy Spirit and what a life of purpose in partnership with God actually means. Because all of these things are facets of how the gospel is reflected in us.

Our lives are not our own. We have been called to live for others. We have been given a commission to embody the character and work of the kingdom to others. No one is left out. No one is excluded. Each is uniquely loved. God wants to reconcile all things to Himself by equipping us to be carriers of His love (see Col. 1:20).

Turn the cup of your life the right way up, so it can be filled afresh and overflow. You can become a carrier of the presence of God.

How does God want to renew the patterns of your thinking so that you are equipped to be a carrier of His love?

For further information, visit www.ffald-y-brenin.org, or go to Roy's website, www.roygodwin.org, for additional resources, including study material such as The Blessings Course.

Chapter 4

THE INSTRUCTED HEART

Caleb has been a hugely important biblical character for me ever since our first few months at Ffald y Brenin. I love his heart, his courage, his trust, his different spirit; the way God Himself testifies and says that Caleb followed Him wholeheartedly. That's how I want to live with every atom of my being. It's not surprising then that as we drafted a declaration of who we are and what our values are that we desired to use the name 'Caleb'.

We originally added the word 'community' but that seemed to imply more than we could offer, such as pastoral care. That is not our role and anyway, we wouldn't have the capacity to deliver. We do not want to disappoint people by promising the impossible. We left Caleb behind and trialed Sheepfold Link, but somehow we weren't comfortable. So in 2016 we turned almost full circle, listened to God and one another some more and launched it as The Caleb Connection.

Like many things at Ffald y Brenin, we had never wished to create a community at all, whether resident or dispersed; in God's timing it gradually emerged. Even when dozens of people raised their longing we had always said no. I had no desire to lead anything—in fact, far from it—and no intention that anything should be centred on Ffald y Brenin.

Yet over time we had to accept that the Lord was directing our steps in what seemed to us a rather undesired direction. But God! Like Joshua who spoke, 'As for me and my house …', we are committed to following the Lord with faith, trust and obedience; wherever He leads we will follow. So we reluctantly but obediently began to look at what it might mean and how we could respond and resource it.

We were not short of material; over the years we had clarified our vision, our values and our growing understanding of our rootedness in what God had done in church history. We recognised that we were a new shoot growing out from a very old root indeed. We began to formulate the basics that might form the expression of the building blocks, the ethos, of whom the Lord has made us to be.

So what exactly is The Caleb Connection, I hear you ask! This book is not the place, nor does it offer the scope, to go into all the detail, but here are some examples of what was produced and it is more alive for us today than ever before.

The Caleb Connection is a dispersed, supportive network that is part of the Ffald y Brenin family. We are not only united by a common vision or by practices alone but by a mutual relationship that is founded on a collection of shared values. These values affect the way we live out our lives. For instance, we value the invitation to truly engage with Jesus and learn what it means to be with Him and become like Him. We seek the King and His kingdom above all else, reveling in the Father's amazing and lavish healing love which He delights to pour out on us by never-ending bucket-loads.

We value being entrusted as stewards of all that we have earlier named as our possessions, our resources and wealth, our assets, our energy, our time and rename them all as His; we offer them to Him and rejoice in the opportunity to serve His purposes in every possible and balanced way. We value people, placing them higher in importance than our projects. We will follow the example of Jesus in always stopping what we are doing in order to be present for the one person in front of us.

We value weakness, not seeking to hide it or hide from it; we acknowledge it, trusting that in it the Lord's own strength might be made perfect. We value the person who most strongly disagrees with our most dearly held views, accepting that the Lord Himself might be speaking through them to us. We renounce the use of power, manipulation or domination in order to get others to do what we want. Instead, we want to become lower, dying to our flesh and being found as servants, just as Jesus was.

We value wasting our time on being with Him, counting it as the best investment we could ever make. We value a thankful heart, an attitude in life that stems from a genuine relationship with God that causes us to become thankful. As we see Him more clearly we see ourselves more clearly, reflected in His gaze, and discover that we are made to be of huge value by His will and totally undeserved love, how can we be anything but thankful?

And so we go on ...

In recent decades people have started to talk about work/life balance as if it was a new concept. In our church traditions we've actually been exploring this for hundreds of years. Benedictine monasticism created a rhythm of life that consisted of prayer, work, study and rest.

But some of these traditions, even in their helpful promotion of life-giving patterns, were still prone to value or affirm a kind of heroic exhaustion as being what God wants. Even today you hear people preaching in this kind of way. There was and is a fear of idleness.

Through The Caleb Connection we offer people the opportunity to step into a rather different pattern and ethos, a lifestyle that sets us free, instead of driving us unhealthily. As we sometimes say in our Rhythm of Daily Prayer, we have been delivered from being driven people, and been made people who are instead led by a Good Shepherd. He leads us out of our uncomfortable, sometimes religious yokes, and puts us where Jesus wants us to be: the place of joy, where the easy, perfectly fitting yoke is available and where the burdens are so light.

> 'Are you tired? Worn out? Burned out on religion?
> Come to me. Get away with me and you'll recover
> your life. I'll show you how to take a real rest. Walk
> with me and work with me—watch how I do it.
> Learn the unforced rhythms of grace. I won't lay
> anything heavy or ill-fitting on you. Keep company
> with me and you'll learn to live freely and lightly'.
> (Matt. 11:28 THE MESSAGE)

So what are these Caleb rhythms that we speak of?

The Rhythm of Prayer

It can be extremely liberating to understand our heavenly Father, the great I AM, as the person He really is rather than viewing Him as an abstract concept. The danger with viewing God as a concept is that we might find ourselves worshipping an idol that we have fashioned ourselves and then find ourselves unwittingly becoming warped by the experience. But the more we get to know Him, the God and Father of our Lord Jesus Christ, the more we will want to know Him and be with Him.

Jesus chose the disciples by inviting them to be with Him, and that is still His desire and invitation for you and me as well. We want to be among those whose heartfelt response is to say with amazement and delight, Yes Lord!

We understand that He has made every one of us to be unique and within that uniqueness we should be able to discover a pattern, a rhythm, of worship, Bible study and prayer that suits us. Our Maker, who has a desire to join us and lavish His time and attention on us, has built that rhythm within us. Do you realise just how much He delights in you and how much joy floods His heart every time He looks at you? Here is love, wide as the ocean, loving-kindness as the sea …

At Ffald y Brenin we have a framework, our Rhythm of Daily Prayer, which helps us and our guests as we meet together to come into His presence four times each day. Sometimes it is sheer joy to go to the meeting place and at other times we discipline ourselves because as long as we are clothed with mortal flesh our moods will be un-predictable. God already understands that—He made us—so there is no problem there. We are surprised by the thousands of copies that have been purchased from around the world and the testimonies of blessing we receive as a result, but there is no demand or imposition upon anyone that they should use it or meet four times daily. If it is right and possible, go for it, and if it isn't, do something else. But do something!

Daphne reads the Bible as soon as she awakes and then goes for a brisk walk while she prays. I usually play worship loudly and have breakfast ready for her return because I am useless first thing in the morning. She would struggle with the sound of praise so early. We are different to each other and that's Ok, an expression of our individuality, our unique make-up. Religion instructs us to get up early and pray; that works well for many but would be a ridiculous burden for others, placing a destructive law upon them.

But however you are made temperamentally and whatever your lifestyle, you need to find a pattern, a regular rhythm, that works for you and gives space to worship, praying, reading the Bible and having time to listen to Him.

How can we minister blessing if we have not been into the tent of meeting? To be a people who are walking in the Way of Blessing demands that we expend time with Him.

The Rhythm of Work

In the formation of structured living going back to early monastic life, the category labelled work included a large range of activity. It might be the physical or intellectual work that enabled the monastery to function and an economy to survive; it might be the time spent in timetabled worship and prayer; it could be the caring for the poor, the sick and the dying; it might be the exercise of a Christian ministry. All this was labelled as work as opposed to rest. We agree because we find it helpful.

When we look at the opening of the Old Testament in the very first chapter of Genesis (which means 'in the beginning' in Hebrew) we read in the very first verse that God was working. We carry on and see something of His work in creation and we soon read of His plan to work in redemption. Jesus spoke in John 5:17 of the Father who is working until now, and He was working. In 2 Corinthians 6:1 Paul wrote that he was working together with Him, not just through Him.

We are designed to be imitators of God; yes, we are marred, bruised, wounded by many a battle, yet still bearing His image. So we are invited to work, and we value it, believing that it has a redemptive and life-fashioning role in our lives. We do all things as for Him who has done all things for us, and given His life as a ransom for many.

The Rhythm of Study

We want to grow and develop in every aspect of our humanity, bearing the image of our Maker through and through like a block of seaside rock, and wisdom and understanding about how to live can be enhanced by learning more about the world around us and the things that interest us or capture our imagination.

The rhythm of study is not confined to Bible-related material although it remains a significant focus. We encourage people to do more than read their Bible prayerfully. We encourage them to study it as well; to get to grips with some of the text. Some will feel more comfortable than others doing that and might enrich others with their insights. But we also want to encourage people to engage with the wider world and see what's going on around them. If they have interests or hobbies, we encourage them to learn more about those areas.

The great Bible teacher John Stott was a skilled photographer and ornithologist (bird watcher). He both found rest and pleasure in this hobby at his cliff-top home near to us. But he also found a deep and profound understanding of the beauty of creation and the wonder of what God had done within it. We want to try and encourage people to see that God has given them the ability to learn and to grow, intellectually as well as socially and spiritually, and that it's a good and positive thing to do so. It's quite clear that Paul knew the words of the poets and quotes them in Acts 17. In Colossians when he refers to the great mystery, he's critiquing the mystery religions of that town. He's very aware of what's going on around him. We want to be aware of what is going on around us.

The bookstall at the Centre is a small model of the rhythm of study. When people are away at a retreat centre they often pray, reflect, walk and fellowship with others. All of these things are part of their stepping out of their ordinary routine to focus on God. Because the phone signal is so poor at our Centre and that distraction is not available, they often read. They have time to read whole books and also to process what they read and internalise it as part of their understanding of what it means to be a disciple and live in the world as an imitator of Jesus.

The Rhythm of Recreation

We rejoice in our understanding that fun, laughter, eating and drinking are good. Enjoying other people for their own sake is good. The world is good—God created a good world. Part of being a whole person is the facility and joy of interacting with other people and enjoying their company.

When Jesus came, one of the criticisms made of Him was how much He seemed to enjoy the world. Well, He should have done so; He created it, so He's reveling in and engaging with His own creation. We are invited to have the same mind.

God has given us the ability to enjoy recreation and it forms an important part within our humanity. Recreation is more than rest. The question we ask people, and particularly busy and dedicated people, is, what do you do for sheer fun or enjoyment that causes you joy? That truly energises you?

Several years ago a visitor asked whether I could spare him a few minutes and although I was very busy I said that I could; people before projects. To my surprise he took me out to the car park and showed me his pride and joy, a small sports car. He invited me to climb into the driver's seat, which I did, and then passed me the keys.

Start her up, he said, and see what it sounds like. After I did that, he invited me to drive the car into the valley. He overrode my objections and insisted that I do so, and reluctantly I drove into the valley and along the lane for a while.

When we returned to the car park he looked at me and asked how long it was since I had driven a car and grinned like a Cheshire cat! It turned out that he had been given about a year to live. He realised that he'd been too busy doing the things of life to actually enjoy living and that it was almost too late.

Apparently he had always had a dream of winning a genuine motor race; this manufacturer arranged single-model races, which offered him a possibility of fulfilling his dream. It took time, training, energy and money, but he did it for sheer exhilaration. He looked at me and asked genuinely whether I was leaving it too late; apparently he was aware of my love for classic sports cars.

It might not have anything to do with driving, but what do you do for the sheer fun of it, the exhilaration that brings you joy and energises you? If you're not sure, why not ask the Lord to show you? If you do know, take pleasure in knowing that God enjoys you doing it!

Everybody's life is of course going to look very different to everybody else's. Some people are very sociable and very active. They want to get out and enjoy their recreation. For other people, they may be more introverted; perhaps they're not so adept socially. They could be living in a place where it's not very easy to have friends around them because they're living in an isolated situation; they will need to find their recreation in other ways.

Any one of these rhythms can take over and unbalance the rest of our lives. For those who are caught up in recreation, it's easy to make recreation so busy that all we have time to do is sleep, work, play, and then get up and start again. We need balance, but more about that shortly.

The Rhythm of Rest

We're not to view heroic exhaustion as pleasing to God; we do need rest. Rest includes sleep, but it is more than that.

Restfulness includes the understanding that God makes no performance demands of us. It includes the understanding that it's the *first* day of the week that is the day of rest. It's not about a day of rest or recovery after we've worked, but a starting point when we can experience the rest that then enables us to go out and work.

The whole principle of understanding rest and of being a people of rest and entering into the Father's rest is based on this: 'It's all done and completed and I am utterly secure because of my Father's acceptance of me. I cannot do anything to win His approval because He's already approved of me. I can't do anything to win His love because He loves me already'. Our Christian culture can lead us to believe the opposite, so that we are forever trying to meet ever-growing demands. Therefore, taking hold of this truth is vital if we are to serve out of an overflow of rest, joy and wonder, rather than from a place of guilt.

There's something else that is very difficult for many and that's the ability to be at rest with ourselves. That can be very challenging. So I find it very interesting to invite people to go and spend perhaps eight hours on their own somewhere, totally isolated from anybody else. I then have them come back the next week to describe their experience. One or all of them will say they found it absolutely horrific and found themselves feeling quite tormented by being alone for that long and that they couldn't cope very well. It's the aloneness that is the issue. It wasn't that they were desperate to see someone else; it was that they couldn't cope with the aloneness. We need to learn to be able to be at rest with ourselves.

Very often a deep operation with the Holy Spirit has to take place in order that we might have that peace and rest with ourselves.

So often we find that the hardest person to be at peace with is ourselves. We can forgive others but we find it so much harder to forgive ourselves. We accept others, with all their history and foibles, but find it so hard to accept ourselves. Our muddled thinking, our sins and secret imaginings all crowd to the fore leaving us oppressed or even fearful. Some struggle with suicidal thoughts after only a few hours on their own. I should know; I had been there and dwelt there for years.

True rest includes entering into the heart of God and His declaration over us. I am chosen, loved and accepted. I have sinned in thought, word and deed and in what I have done and failed to do. Yet still He chooses to forgive me, cleanse me, accept me; I find myself in the place of the prodigal who looks at himself so realistically and yet is interrupted by a father who is crazily in love with him; confessions, apologies, all swept away in a torrent of embraces and welcome.

In saying that he was not worthy, he identified with his own honest self-evaluation, his personal understanding of the situation. Yet the father embraced him in spite of the stench of sin and gave him a totally unexpected status that flew in the face of all that anyone would have expected.

That's how He has treated me; and not only me, but actually every child who has come home to Him. We are so slow to recognise it, but it's the undeserved truth.

Once the party was over I bet the prodigal son had the best night's sleep for many a long day. He was at home. Welcomed; forgiven; accepted; the smell of sin washed away, the past swept away and his sinful heart healed. You are that son, as am I; the same welcome is offered to us both.

As well as the Caleb rhythm we have other 'habits of the heart' that help shape our community.

Let's examine what these habits include …

A Heart of Thankfulness: Living a Life of Joyful Celebration

We want to be people who are shaped by thankfulness and gratitude; people who find it easy to say thank you to God and who carry an attitude of thankfulness throughout their daily lives. This is all rooted in a massive thread in the tapestry of grace.

The Hebrew people believed that Yahweh was consistent, gracious and merciful. The other religions of the day often worshipped gods who were inconsistent, immoral, vengeful and unforgiving. The followers of these pagan gods were involved in a transaction—I prayed my prayer or offered my sacrifice, so now give me what I want. The people of Israel were different. They had a relational God whose steadfast love they celebrated. They enjoyed His creation and so they gave thanks. They prayed a prayer every afternoon that had eighteen verses of thankfulness.

Many of the epistles open with prayers of thanks and Jesus thanked the Father for food, revelation for the poor and marginal and much else.

Paul stands in that tradition when he commends a rhythm of thankfulness:

> Let the peace of Christ rule in your hearts, since as members of one body you were called to peace. And be thankful. Let the message of Christ dwell among you richly as you teach and admonish one another with all wisdom through psalms, hymns, and songs from the Spirit, singing to God with gratitude in your hearts.

And whatever you do, whether in word or deed, do it
all in the name of the Lord Jesus, giving thanks to God
the Father through him. (Col. 3:15-17)

This thankfulness then leads on to a life of joyful celebration. Because we're chosen, adopted and loved and graced with the Holy Spirit and have an inheritance that can't be shaken and we're walking in a foretaste of it now, we want to be people who find it easy to celebrate. At Ffald y Brenin we celebrate just about anything we can think of that can be celebrated: birthdays, anniversaries and much more. Celebration for us generally involves food! We might sing sometimes and we'll laugh together, and we will have lots of fun celebrating.

We want to be people who are looking forward to the marriage supper of the Lamb, who celebrate the fact that we have been made children of God. We want to reflect this attitude of celebration in all that we do as well as deliberately celebrating when milestones are reached in all our lives. There's something in this communal joy that not only makes us more whole but also testifies to what God has done within us as well.

It echoes the promises of God too. The Father and Jesus love celebrating. Isaiah 25:6 tells us that one day 'the Lord Almighty will prepare a feast of rich food for all peoples, a banquet of aged wine—the best of meats and the finest of wines'. The Bible contains numerous stories and parables that support the revelation that there is going to be a lot of feasting in the age to come.

When we celebrate the Lord's Supper, the Eucharist, it's often hard to discern in what way it might truthfully be declared a celebration at all. We seem to interpret the instruction of Jesus to remember Him as being a heavy and oppressive thing. The tendency so easily arises to lean into the religious instead of the life. When we consider the battlefield of Calvary we are overawed, but we don't stop there.

If we did there would be plenty of cause to mourn. Failed hope, no gospel. But we remember His triumph, and empty cross, and empty grave and an occupied throne in heaven. We remember not only that we are saved at enormous cost, but that we are saved right now! How can we fail to celebrate and be thankful?

Jesus worked His first public miracle at a wedding feast when He changed water into wine. He told a parable about a banquet where people were invited in from among the most marginal groups of the day. He fed 5,000 in a foretaste of the marriage supper of the Lamb. He cooked fish for His disciples after the resurrection. And He ate with all the wrong people—especially tax collectors—all the time. To say that He shocked the religious people of the time would be an understatement. Jesus would feel totally at home at our own celebrations.

Being Shaped by Simplicity

What's the purpose of my life but to know Him and to seek the kingdom of God and His righteousness before anything else? Therefore all the other things that I have in my life have to be subservient to that. They have to be a servant to my kingdom focus. I'm not going to be a slave to anything except Jesus and His kingdom. So there's going to be simplicity in the way that I live, which means that in practical terms I will always be focused on the goal.

Mention simplicity and we often interpret it as poverty, yet that is not what we are suggesting; it's simplicity. I'm going to live in a simple way and my attitude is going to be simple. What we mean is that absolutely everything in life must be measured and valued in accordance with the surpassing value of the kingdom of God. It is the treasure in my field, the pearl of great price.

That might and should touch my financial situation, in that if I really don't have very much in terms of money, then how much more am I going to value my family, my relationships. I'm going to be living in simplicity, trusting and pursuing Him. But if I have been enabled to have an abundant supply of money, enough for my needs and more then I thank the Lord and recognise the responsibility that comes with having what I have. Our watchword in respect to this will be, 'I don't own this, I steward it and it's for the King and His kingdom and His purposes and values'.

Remaining Engaged with Mission

Loving God, serving others. Four powerful words, rich in meaning. Out of our love for God, as an imitation of Him, rooted in seeing our lives as acts of worship, we serve and bless our communities. Being a blessing is about our character, rooted in God's character, being an avenue for the Holy Spirit to work and act in the lives of those we are in contact with, in order to bring glory to Jesus.

This will include releasing acts that bless. The street pastors who give flip-flops to drunk girls for their walk home bless entire communities. Sprained ankles as a result of falling off their high-heeled shoes can cause a cost of £40,000 to the local hospitals, the workplace and the person themselves. A simple act of kindness benefits everybody, not just the recipient. It is an act that blesses.

The story of a man who wheeled the bin for his frail neighbour is a perfect picture of acts that bless. I know of a man who lived in a cul-de-sac. He didn't know anybody and he didn't know what he could do to connect with the people who lived there. One evening he was taking his wheeled rubbish bin to the entrance of his drive ready for collection the next morning. He looked across and saw an elderly gentleman, diagonally opposite, also slowly wheeling his bin to his gate.

He thought he'd go across and say hello. He went over and introduced himself. They had lived there for many years but had never met each other. They chatted for a bit and then he suddenly had a thought and said, 'I'd better be going back, but let me take your wheelie bin for you'.

The elderly man was very grateful and explained why. His wife was an invalid and was quite ill. He had experienced a number of heart attacks and every time he went out to move the wheelie bin, she worried that he might over-exert himself. She would lose him and also be very vulnerable herself.

My friend told him that he would do the bin for him from now on. The old man was amazed and quite emotional that anybody should bother to help him. In its most simple form this mundane act of kindness was releasing an act that blessed that man and his wife.

When we act in this way people talk and they say, 'You'd never guess what happened'? Eventually they ask, 'Why are you acting like this'? Or they perceive something in you that provokes trust and are more comfortable to talk about their life challenges and their spiritual questions. It's sometimes called permission evangelism. People ask you to tell them about your story and your beliefs. They give you permission.

Witnessing to them of the saving power of Jesus Christ is the greatest blessing we can ever bring to someone. We gain a right to be heard by the lives that we live but the time comes when we have to name the Name: Jesus!

My friend reacted as he did because it had become second nature to him to help others. The things that we do instinctively arise from deeply ingrained attitudes and these arise from the habits of the heart that hold sway in the patterns of our thinking.

Loving our neighbour as ourselves includes the person that we are leading to the Lord out of a non-Christian lifestyle. For instance, the unsaved person who is living with a partner—people who live as if they were married, despite not having made the covenant before witnesses. If we love our neighbour as ourselves, that person's partner is our neighbour, as well as the person we are leading to the Lord.

We have a choice of being legalistic and saying, this is wrong, you'd better stop: or of loving both parties as we love ourselves and committing them to the Lord without placing a judgment on them. Leading the one to the Lord and trusting that the Holy Spirit will lead them both into truth and change their lives is the Way of Blessing. It depends upon mercy triumphing over judgment.

I'm aware at the moment of someone who wants to become a Christian, but cannot get over the barrier of the people who are saying they can't until they leave their partner, and they can't cope with that. Well, it's putting the cart before the horse. I feel brokenhearted for that person who can't come as they are to the Lord. Everything will be different and the hard situations people are in will begin to change once Jesus is in the equation.

In the Benedictine monastic tradition they speak of two aspects of salvation. There is conversion of heart, which we'd understand as conversion or being born again, followed by conversion of life. The conversion of life doesn't always move at the same speed in every life. Being patient while people's lives catch up is not compromise—it's grace.

Remembering the Poor

We worship a generous God who calls us to be like Him and become generous. If we begin to look at what's going on in the world in terms of natural disasters, refugees, infectious disease and so on we simply cannot meet the world's needs out of our own pocket however generous we are. Therefore we can become people who feel guilty if we don't give to every appeal we ever come across. If we're Christians how can we say no?

We suggest to people that they make a budget for their lives generally and then create a budget for giving. I cannot meet everybody's needs, but are there those whose needs I can do something about? Might I be a regular giver?

Why not make a plan and say this is where, and how much, I give. If someone comes along and asks if we can give to something else, we might be able to say yes but we can also say, 'Actually I have a budget and I'm already committed'. It helps to lift the sense of guilt and burden.

Secondly, why not have a pot in which we stick in a bit of spare money now and again. If there's an emergency that arises, there's an amount of money sitting in the pot and we can give it without trying to dig deeper into our resources, if that's the right thing to do.

Jesus and the disciples had a fund for the poor. Judas was offended when someone lavished expensive perfume on the feet of Jesus because in his view the money could have gone in the poor fund. The early church had a fund for the poor, which is described in Acts 4. People could be in hardship because of a poor harvest, a tax demand that emptied their coffers or their being shunned by their natural family because of their decision to follow the teaching of Jesus.

It was a habitual choice, a key value of the followers of Jesus that they remembered the poor. The book of James warns about neglecting them and favouring the rich. In chapter 11 of his first letter to the Corinthians, Paul suggests that their neglect of the poor is a desecration of one of the implicit messages of the Communion meal: that all who sat there were equal before the Father.

Having said that, when we think of remembering the poor, we tend to instinctively think about what money we can give. How about making that the second thought instead? How about making the first thought, what could I do? Is there some *thing* I can do? Could I give time, thought, energy to be a blessing rather than only a money-giver? But don't forget to give money as well.

Rather than just thinking about people in far-off lands, what about the poor in our own community? What about those struggling economically? What about those who are having their goods confiscated or facing bankruptcy? What about single parents who are denying themselves to feed and clothe their children? Who are the poor where we are? To bless is to play a part in the story.

A Life on the Way of Blessing

We desire to be those upon whose lips the fragrant praises of Jesus' name are found, and who breathe out effective blessings in His magnificent and powerful name as easily and naturally as we inhale the air around us. God's presence will go before us and surround us when we do.

How have we seen His presence at work at Ffald y Brenin?

For further information, visit www.ffald-y-brenin.org, or go to Roy's website, www.roygodwin.org, for additional resources, including study material such as The Blessings Course.

Chapter 5

BLESSING AND THE PRESENCE OF GOD

Rachel was dreaming. Dreaming of two people inviting her to get up out of her wheelchair. Dreaming that her strength would be restored. It would not be long before the dream became reality. Understanding that healing is in the good and wonderful purpose of God is one thing. But the intellectual assent moves to active faith when we get a revelation that this truth is for us. Rachel's revelation would bear fruit before the sun set again during their much-anticipated holiday.

John and Rachel Wigram had come on holiday to North Pembrokeshire with their teenage children. They were in a caravan near the lighthouse a few miles from Ffald y Brenin. John and Rachel are ordained in the Anglican Church.

Rachel had suffered from ME for thirty-two years and for the last six years it had been very severe meaning that she had to spend her time in virtual isolation in one room in one chair, often with the curtains closed. She was unable to get out and about at all without being pushed in a wheelchair. People in a neighbouring caravan suggested that a drive through the Gwaun Valley might be possible for her and so, one day, John took her there. The need for a disabled toilet took them to a car park at the bottom of a drive that was marked as 'Ffald y Brenin Christian Retreat Centre'.

It took them a while to realise why it sounded familiar. A friend had read *The Grace Outpouring* a while before and had expressed a longing that Rachel might be able to get there somehow but had no idea how that could happen. They knew very little about it but thought that it couldn't be a mere coincidence that they had ended up there. So, John called our number and asked if it might be possible to visit and to meet Daphne and myself, but he was very concerned about accessibility and whether it would be too much for his wife.

Daphne sensed God saying that there would be a positive outcome. The timetable the next day went a bit awry for all of us and when we eventually saw them they had been sitting in the prayer room for over an hour—there was nowhere else they could go with the wheelchair.

We walked across and opened the door. Daphne and I looked at each other and we grinned, because the manifest presence of God was there. We greeted them and talked a little. Then I said to Rachel, 'This is your time. This is your day', and I asked her, 'Do you want to be healed'?

That morning before coming, Rachel had written in her journal, 'What do I want? I want to meet the risen Jesus. I want to believe and not doubt. I want to be really healed from ME Could it possibly be my time, my day—God's time, God's day for me'?

My words echoed what she had written and stirred faith in her and she replied, 'What must I do'? We took a hand each and said to her, 'In the name of Jesus, stand up'! We helped her and she stood up and we held on to her as she got her balance. Then she took one step and then another and soon she was off around the room, leaping and dancing and laughing for joy as energy surged through her body.

Daphne, being Daphne, fetched an adult-size multi-coloured skipping rope, and said, 'Try that'! Rachel did start skipping and then she went over to her husband and they hugged each other. They were laughing, crying and trembling. I felt a little tug in my mind. God told me they were literally in shock and John particularly needed a cup of tea and a moment of calm. Rachel, who hadn't been able to make tea for her husband for years, demanded she make it, despite the tricky steps between there and the kitchen. They sat there laughing, crying and drinking tea.

We were minutes away from midday prayer, held in the summer in the prayer room because of all the day visitors. We removed the cross, candles and communion items from the table. Then we folded the wheelchair and put it on top of the table with the open Bible with the cross on the top.

People were curious about the table but I said nothing for a while before inviting an explanation. Rachel, with John not far behind her, jumped up and explained that this was her wheelchair, which had held her captive for years. The place erupted with praise, thanksgiving and worship, tears and laughter as Rachel walked around the room.

The fruit was both highly practical and quite profound. That evening, with their amazed children, they walked to the lighthouse together as a family. Back home, her dentist and receptionist were shocked when their wheelchair-bound patient walked in. Her GP had never seen her on her feet and was overjoyed as she explained what had happened. She came out from behind the desk and threw her arms around her in celebration, remarking that it sounded just like a Bible story. Now, three and a half years later, she is living a full and active life, leading a church with John and they have fulfilled their dream of walking some of the Pembrokeshire coast path as a family.

Although they were far from home Jesus had to come to the Wigrams' world that day, in the same way that He came to a house in Capernaum. Mark 2:1-12 tells us:

> A few days later, when Jesus again entered Capernaum, the people heard that he had come home. They gathered in such large numbers that there was no room left, not even outside the door, and he preached the word to them. Some men came, bringing to Him a paralysed man, carried by four of them. Since they could not get him to Jesus because of the crowd, they made an opening in the roof above Jesus by digging through it and then lowered the mat the man was lying on. When Jesus saw their faith, he said to the paralysed man, 'Son, your sins are forgiven'.
>
> Now some teachers of the law were sitting there, thinking to themselves, 'Why does this fellow talk like that? He's blaspheming! Who can forgive sins but God alone'?
>
> Immediately Jesus knew in his spirit that this was what they were thinking in their hearts, and he

said to them, 'Why are you thinking these things?
Which is easier: to say to this paralysed man, 'Your
sins are forgiven', or to say, 'Get up, take your mat
and walk'? But I want you to know that the Son of
Man has authority on earth to forgive sins'. So he
said to the man, 'I tell you, get up, take your mat
and go home'. He got up, took his mat and walked
out in full view of them all. This amazed everyone
and they praised God, saying, 'We have never seen
anything like this'!

Jesus was in the house, preaching the word to them. But as we
will discover throughout the chapters that follow there is an aspect of
salvation that is like the twin of forgiveness—healing.

In the midst of the crowded, hot, tumultuous streets come four
friends carrying a sick man. They were getting ready to intercede
with Jesus for the health of their friend.

Rachel had three friends bringing her to Jesus for healing. The
friend who phoned her husband, Robert; Robert, who brought her
to the Centre and the Holy Spirit, who had shown Robert where the
Centre was and given Rachel a dream of what the next day would
bring. Their entry was not easy either, waiting in a room, because
the terrain was not easy for someone in a wheelchair. But God met
with her that day in a way that she could have hardly dreamt of
twenty-four hours before. The man sick with palsy was also surprised
by grace, mercy, love, and healing.

At the heart of what God has been doing among us is a belief
that Jesus left heaven to be 'in the house' here with us on earth. He

brought heaven near to us and empowered us by the Holy Spirit to bring heaven near to others.

Much of the way that He talks of the work of the kingdom involves pictures of proximity:

> 'The time has come', he said. 'The **kingdom of God** has come near. Repent and believe the good news'! Mark 1:15

> Heal those there who are ill and tell them, 'The **kingdom of God** has come near to you'. Luke 10:9

> Once, on being asked by the Pharisees when the kingdom of God would come, Jesus replied, 'The coming of the kingdom of God is not something that can be observed, nor will people say, "Here it is," or "There it is," because the kingdom of God is in your midst'. Luke 17:20-21

We came to realise that we could have programmes, meetings, and crusades but actually more than anything we needed Jesus to be 'in the house'. What do we mean by this? Isaiah 40:11-12 reminds us that we worship a God who is present in a majestic way in all creation but also profoundly cares for individuals within that creation.

> He tends his flock like a shepherd:
> he gathers the lambs in his arms

and carries them close to his heart;
he gently leads those that have young.

Who has measured the waters in the hollow of
        his hand,
or with the breadth of his hand marked off the
        heavens?
Who has held the dust of the earth in a basket,
or weighed the mountains on the scales
and the hills in a balance?

In the midst of God's impossible-to-measure majesty He draws near to us. He sends Jesus to come near to the broken and wounded, the sinful and the saints. His presence is manifest in compassion, healing, forgiveness, and the calming of nature and His return from death.

In this story of the four friends and the sick man we find other clues that business as usual has been suspended. The appearance of the glory of God amidst a throng of singing angels and in the presence of lowly shepherds was a first clue. The presence of God was identified with the temple and here it was in the countryside. Forgiveness was sought at the temple and here was Jesus offering it to a sick man, in a small town, on a mat, in a crowded room, littered with bits of roof. The religious onlookers felt their story unraveling, their power slipping away. The manifest presence of God was leaving the temple, residing in Jesus and would be placed on His disciples that they might carry it to the ends of the earth.

But Jesus discerned their thoughts and tells them, 'The son of man has authority on earth to forgive sins'. But salvation and healing are never too far from each other when Jesus enters a house. Jesus says to the sick man, 'I tell you arise'. The word used here speaks of awakening.

Jesus says, 'Take your mat'. This was symbol of the illness that had captured the paralytic. It no longer held him. He carried it away. He was reigning over it. Out of his brokenness he was strengthened for compassion; out of his pain he could help others step out of brokenness. Carrying his bed, how many people might stop him and ask what he was doing, which opened a wonderful opportunity to testify.

There is more truth for us in this passage and its place in the unfolding of the kingdom. Jesus delegates the authority that He has claimed to seventy of His disciples, just as Moses had done to the seventy God gave him, breathed on them that might receive the Holy Spirit and sends them out to exercise authority in His name and bring the kingdom of God near to people (see Luke 10).

When the presence of God is among us we too should expect extraordinary miracles.

It was a Prayer Day and we were praying for many people. I noticed a particular lady and sensed God wanted Daphne and me to minister to that particular woman: she needed some people with more experience. She agreed with Daphne that we could pray for her. She stood in front of us, put her head down, then looked up at both of us in turn and tried to speak, but couldn't.

I asked her if she would like me to step away and leave her with Daphne. She indicated that it was fine for me to stay. That enabled her to begin to speak and she sobbed deeply and then said that she had suffered repeated sexual assaults since infanthood, resulting in cancer.

We had a word for her and the Holy Spirit came upon her very powerfully and she sank to the floor. We knelt down and spoke a few words over her life, blessed her and then moved on. Eventually she returned to her seat.

About a week later we had a phone call from her. The team members were struggling to deal with her and she was asking to speak to me. She didn't seem coherent so I told her that I was going to pray for God's help and then I blessed her in the name of Jesus, that the peace of God would fall upon her. All the sound stopped and I heard a deep exhalation and she said, 'Thank goodness, thank You, Lord, that's what I needed'.

She told me enough that I then knew who she was. After she had sat down that day God had prompted her to go outside and check her colostomy bag. (We hadn't known she had one.) She ignored the prompting, convinced that it was not God and after the fourth time asked God to stop whatever voice it was.

Chrissie, who we met in the first chapter, took her home and Ruth settled into her evening routine, which included checking her colostomy bag. It was crystal clean, hanging in its right place on its ribbons, but it wasn't plugged in. She was really concerned, because try as she might it would not plug back in. She didn't know who she could call at that time of night, so despite her worry she went to bed.

She rang the surgery the first thing in the morning and they told her to come straight in. She was taken in to see the GP who knows her well and had been involved in arranging all the many operations she had experienced. He started to examine her and then gasped—there was no flap and no mark, no scar or anything, only perfect skin.

They soon realised that the scars from her all her operations had gone. Even the scar from her caesarean from when she was a young woman had also gone and she had beautiful, clear skin.

The doctor didn't know what to do so he rang the hospital there and then and got through to the surgeon's secretary. They instructed him to bring her straightaway. The surgeon and his team examined her and then she had a scan. She was discharged with the promise of a letter about what they had found.

The surgeon noted that she been referred from the GP because she had sensed significant changes in her body. The letter, of which we have a copy, confirmed that her intuition was correct. Her bowel, which had been deemed irredeemable had been rectified, was functioning normally. It noted that the team had no explanation to offer as to what has taken place but that something definitely had.

This was an extraordinary miracle, which would be the start of the healing of every aspect of her life.

It's inspiring to see the glory of God leave the temple of our meetings or expectations and do His work. Jesus can be 'in the house' in your home, your workplace or on the streets. The scripture reminds us that:

> Therefore submit to God. Resist the devil and he will
> flee from you. Draw near to God and He will draw
> near to you. Cleanse *your* hands, *you* sinners; and
> purify *your* hearts, *you* double-minded. (James 4:7-8)

We seek to draw near to God as part of our daily practice at Ffald y Brenin with prayer and reflection at least four times a day. We should not be surprised if He draws near to us and we find our surroundings becoming what is a thin place. In that context we are often merely guideposts for people, rather than at the heart of what God does within them. We bring wisdom and direction but the Spirit does the work. Jesus is in the house, or our street, in our workplace or our club, in our church or small group and we are there to help or explain what He is doing.

We had a New Age traveller guest at Ffald y Brenin. She told me very clearly that she hated Christians because of our claim that Jesus was the only way to God. I agreed with her, which she found surprising, but said that what was really important was not what we said at all, but what Jesus said. I advised her to go and talk to Him. She wanted to stay and argue. The next morning she was hammering on the door. 'Why didn't you tell me? You didn't tell me what I need to know—that Jesus was the Son of God and that He has sent the Holy Spirit'.

Revelation had come as she had read the scripture. The Holy Spirit had brought the words alive. We should not be surprised when the absolutely astonishing happens when we have honoured God with our prayers, our lives and our worship.

We know that God walked with Adam and Eve in the Garden, wrestled with Jacob, sent dreams and visions to Joseph, the man betrothed of Mary. He opened up the mission to the Gentiles in a visionary experience on a rooftop for Peter, the apostle. We should not be surprised if He does the same today.

'Fred' (not his real name) was an older, formal man in his early eighties with an educated accent. He wore a pin-striped suit with a white shirt and tie to our chapel services, so he rather stood out.

He prayed in every meeting. It seemed very formal, like almost every other aspect of his life. But on his final day, a Friday, we noticed that he didn't contribute at morning prayers. As I was leaving to go he got hold of my arm and asked if he could talk to me for a moment and tell me about something that had happened. I wondered, given how he had been, whether he was going to point out a shortcoming in the Centre—perhaps there had not been enough milk that morning for his breakfast cereal!

Fred's story came tumbling out. The previous night, knowing that it was his last evening, he realised he had to go and visit the high cross on the edge of the Ffald y Brenin grounds. The young people of his church had urged him to come to the Centre and also suggested he spend time at the cross. He was not that keen. He knew what the two pieces of wood signified so didn't see why he should bother to walk there. But in the end, despite his reluctance, he decided to walk down the leaf-strewn path so that he could assure the young people he had indeed been to the cross.

Many of the miracles at Ffald y Brenin occur after a cup of tea and this was no exception. His decision made, Fred had a cup of tea and then walked slowly through the avenue of trees, thinking to himself, *This is really silly.* He reached the five-bar gate at the end of the avenue, looking up at the rising ground and there on top was the high cross.

He could see it clearly and felt he had now discharged his duty to the young people. He was about to walk back to his room when he became aware of movement nearby and of someone standing by him. The person was also leaning on the gate, close enough that their elbows touched. This was a little uncomfortable for him and he turned to see who it was.

At this point, Fred broke from his story-telling and looked at me before asking whom I thought it was. I hazarded a guess that it might have been one of the guests.

'It was Jesus', he said. Somehow he had immediately recognised him, perhaps as the disciples on the mountaintop recognised Moses and Elijah. Jesus greeted him and he mumbled a similar greeting back, not knowing the proper etiquette for talking during a theophany. Then they both went back to gazing at the cross again.

But then Jesus asked Fred a question. He asked him what he could remember of the story of Easter. What had happened? He told Him what he remembered. Jesus affirmed his answer and then asked another question that provoked a memory about another way of understanding the Easter story. They settled into a pattern of Jesus asking questions that brought out more answers from the memory of Fred. Another question took him back to when he was about four years old and at pre-school and the memory of something the teacher had said about the cross.

Fred was pretty amazed at what was happening. But it got better from there:

> *Jesus stood by me and took all the answers and took hold of them and in an instant fashioned them into pictorial form, like pieces of a jigsaw and then He locked them together, to make an incredible and beautiful picture of what happened on the cross.*
>
> *But then He took hold of me and put me in the middle of the story. I said, 'That's incredible'. He said, 'That's nothing really'! At that moment He seemed to reach to the core of my being and switch me on.*
>
> *All of my life I have known that I am dead, and all of my life I have known that I am surrounded by people who are so obviously alive. I have never in my life known what it's like to*

*be alive as a person. But now Jesus has switched me on and I
know for the first time that I am alive as well.*

I have to tell you that it was a joy hearing Fred say these things
and to agree with him that Jesus makes us alive because of what has
happened on the cross.

He told me he was a bit upset as well! He added:

*I'm in my early eighties and God makes me alive—what about
all this life I've lived, the whole of my childhood, my youth and
my working life, my early years of retirement, being dead, and
now at this age He makes me alive. Why couldn't He have done
it before?*

It was a joy to share with Fred about that truth: that however
badly we have been robbed of life, when we are responsive to Him
He works His wonders in our life and makes us alive. He is able to
restore to us everything that we have lost and more besides.

I encouraged him. 'In a while you will be able to say, with perfect
integrity, "My story is that I have received more in two years from
the hand of God and I have lived more in those two years than in the
previous eighty-one years of my life." He will restore the years that
have been stolen.'

When Jesus is in the house, when His presence becomes manifest,
we should not be surprised. I have never had any problem believing
that the earth is the Lord's and the fullness thereof, and in spite of
recognising the difficulties and the challenges, I have eyes to see that
the whole world is full of God's glory. I have no difficulty in believing

in the omnipresence of God and the fact that there was nowhere I could go to be away from His presence.

Because of that, I grew up with a distinct attitude of scepticism about the idea of there being any particular places in the world where God was doing a special work. So when I heard of movements like the Toronto Airport Church and the Brownsville Assemblies of God in Pensacola I stayed put. We were never tempted at all, because whatever God was doing we rejoiced in, but the point was, why wouldn't He come and do it here? I think that's a pretty typical evangelical viewpoint.

But after we'd been at Ffald y Brenin for a number of years we began to see that God was doing specific things within the place of Ffald y Brenin. When we asked Him to do some things outside the border people experienced the same things happening outside the border, but in terms of maybe ten or fifteen yards from the border.

Bethel is one of the places that's spoken of as a special place in the Old Testament where God does specific things. Bethlehem is spoken of as being the place where the Messiah would be born. Jerusalem—that is the place where world-shaking events will take place and where the presence of God will be known and celebrated in a special place.

You go up to Jerusalem; you sing the song of Ascents, because when you get there it isn't the same as other places. God has chosen to do something in that place. The Bible also tells us that one day there will be a renewal of the earth and the new Jerusalem will come down. There will be a renewed earth and a new city, new life and structures where there is no need of sun or moon, because the Lamb is in the midst.

I have begun to realise that while the Scriptures point to the fact that God is everywhere and you cannot escape His presence, He also chooses to manifest Himself in a particular way and in a particular place at a particular time.

I guess that when Moses saw the burning bush, it was the only bush that was burning. It was that bush—it was a specific bush. This didn't in anyway diminish the fact that God was everywhere. God tells him, 'Take your shoes off, Moses, this is holy ground'. We're aware that there is a recognition of the manifestation of the holiness of God, and we'd better be careful that we recognise it and are careful as we approach it.

For some that holiness provokes a challenge. Thousands of cars come into the car park at Ffald y Brenin every year. Ever so often the presence of God encounters people in the car park as they arrive.

Two friends had arrived having travelled together. They were chatting away very happily. They were both confessing Christians and were looking forward to their time with us. They parked the car and as the passenger opened the door and her feet touched the ground something happened. A voice that was clearly not her own burst out from her saying, 'What are you doing, what are you doing bringing me here? I'm not allowed here; I have to go; I'm not allowed to be in this place'. It left her with some force.

This stunned and staggered her friend who never had any inclinations that there was anything going on that wasn't good with her friend. The rather startled passenger was totally unaware of what had happened, except for a sudden sense of a freedom and liberty in herself that she hadn't known for a long time.

That's just one story as similar things have happened with a number of people when their feet have touched the ground in the car park. Why does that happen? Our understanding is that as we continuously day by day invite the kingdom of God to fill and break out in this place, by which we mean the government of God, which is a spiritual, not a physical reality, that something is taking place in the heavenly realms. There is something that is holy about the place, the ground, because the Lord is here. It's only because He's here. There's something about the strength of God's rule that is able to confront and expel evil spirits and demonic presences.

Some visitors have a different kind of spiritual encounter. I am not among those who bear witness to having seen angels, but so many guests over the years have shared strikingly similar stories of angelic activity that the reality of it can't be dismissed.

We have had a number of occasions where, particularly in night prayers, there has been a choir outside the chapel windows—a beautiful choir joining in the worship, singing praise, glorifying the Lamb, singing over the chapel, but there's nobody there. They made beautiful music. Guests speak of having seen angels on the hilltops; sometimes worshipping, sometimes praising; almost always looking as though they are waiting to do the Father's bidding.

So, what is our role in sharing the blessings of God and welcoming His presence? How are we to understand the authority we have been given? How does blessing come to places as well as people? How can we be part of God's restoration programme?

For further information, visit www.ffald-y-brenin.org, or go to Roy's website, www.roygodwin.org, for additional resources, including study material such as The Blessings Course.

Chapter 6

IN THE NAME OF JESUS

A motorbike gang rode into a small New Zealand town near Te Puke and parked their bikes; they took their insignia and their jackets off, kicked their bikes over and knelt down in front of the astonished people. They publicly renounced their way of life and pledged to become followers of Jesus.

On another occasion in the business section of town thirty-four members of a criminal gang called Black Power, famous in Australia and New Zealand, arrived *en masse*. This gang was seriously feared and there was genuine distress as people braced themselves for what might happen!

The men knelt on the pavement amongst the people and cried out to Jesus to save them. The Holy Spirit came upon them; twelve months later they had been integrated into small groups and were growing in their faith.

This was not happening in a city or a nation famed for its well-known churches or powerful pastors. Like much of what God does it was starting in an obscure town in the South Pacific nation of New

Zealand, in a distant place. Jesus came from the margins of Israel in Galilee and it seems that God still operates that way today. Here is why the glory of God was touching the streets.

An elder had stood up at church in Te Puke, located on the North Island of New Zealand one Sunday evening and said, 'I'm not going to preach a sermon this evening, I'm going to read you excerpts from a book called *The Grace Outpouring*'. As he read to them about the kingdom of God and blessing, the Holy Spirit began to move amongst the congregation.

At the close of the meeting the elders got together and decided to respond to what they had heard. They sensed a new desperation for the work of the Spirit in their region and felt that they should meet six evenings per week to learn how to be a people of prayer and blessing.

So they started to meet. Eighteen months later it was still continuing—six evenings per week. People had moved into the town to be near the prayer meeting and be accessible if they could; eight local churches had joined in with them. The host church has had to appoint new pastors to help cope with the people who have become Christians in the prayer meeting. There have been waves of praise and blessing and waves of salvation and waves of healing.

One of the elders came from New Zealand to Ffald y Brenin to share the story with us. At an early prayer meeting, the parents of a little child suddenly became aware of their two-year-old crawling across the floor and lying across the feet of a nearby man, praying and simply calling out, 'Jesus'. They think that the youngster continued for about five minutes before crawling off.

The man suddenly yelled and stood up and started walking around. They asked if he was all right. The man had been involved in an accident many years ago and had a deformed foot and constant severe pain. His pain had disappeared, so they looked at the baby and then looked at the man!

They encouraged him to take his shoe off, which he did and discovered he had a perfectly reshaped foot. The man was new to this type of meeting so they took time with him to explain that this was not a magic child, but that the Holy Spirit had done this, through the name of Jesus, and that the toddler had simply prayed for him. The other people there just continued to worship and praise the Lord.

The nearest town, which is actually some distance away, is a major town in the area. A young Mexican girl in her early twenties turned up as she was visiting friends and relatives. She was on fire about Jesus and her experience of Him. One of them asked whether she would go to the high school and share her story at a school gathering. She agreed and was taken to the school and she spoke at the assembly, whereupon the Holy Spirit fell on the school. During that afternoon half the pupils and half the staff publicly responded to the Gospel.

That was a short time after blessings began to be pronounced on a daily basis. The God of plenty had come to the Bay of Plenty in response to those who proclaimed His blessing for that remote New Zealand region.

This story captures something of what happens as the people of God start to pronounce the blessings of God for people and regions.

In a moment I want to share with you the scriptural pattern that provoked us to be a people of blessing but first let us deal with those things that can inhibit us from taking hold of these truths.

Stumbling Blocks to Blessing

It is hard sometimes to orient ourselves toward blessing. We view the world around us through a lens of suspicion. One day a man knocked on our door and said, 'I've just got to thank you for changing our lives. This teaching about blessing has changed everything for us. Fundamentally it has changed us because we are so busy blessing everyone that we have forgotten how to judge them and curse them which is how we used to live'.

Sadly, that is true for a lot of us. We're against things. As Christians we're against this and against that. We object to this and object to that. We speak out *against* things, but how often do we speak out about those things that we are *for*?

The number of Christians who are quick to condemn sin in the world of sinners and demand the judgment of God in retaliation absolutely amazes me. Have we forgotten that the right time for God to send Jesus into the world for you and me was precisely when you and I were lost in our trespasses and sin? The whole meaning of the doctrine of grace is that God has chosen, and is still choosing, to treat us with favour even though we will never ever be able to earn it or deserve it.

God is not caught by surprise when people sin. He expects that sinners will sin and it doesn't catch Him by surprise. Centuries ago, Brother Lawrence was recorded as saying, in *The Practice of the Presence of God*, that God is not surprised that there is sin in the world; if anything, He is surprised that there isn't more.

Surely, sin is what sinners do? Have we forgotten? He's already done something about it by sending Jesus, so He's already acted for them. What's His desire? Is it to swing the axe or call down the fire of God? The disciples talked like that at times but Jesus reminded them that this was not His way. He longs to gather them under His wings.

At times we hear from Christians who believe that we should not pray blessing for people who are not yet Christians. They deserve judgment in their view. The problem with this perspective is that it is simply not reflective of scriptural truth. The shocking command to bless those who curse you is spoken by Jesus and is echoed by Paul (see Luke 6:28; Rom. 12:14). The prophet Jeremiah must have sent a shudder through the exiles when he commended them to seek the prosperity of the place where they lived. They wanted to be back in the holy city and here he was telling them to bring blessing to a heathen city (see Jer. 29:7).

Jesus prays *for* things not *against* them. Jesus brings life, not death. Jesus gives us a mandate to provoke us to be a people of blessing—we will explore that in a few moments.

Sometimes we won't bless people and pray for their healing because it's emotionally safer if we don't try. Jesus did those things but we don't—is the inner conversation we have. But as we have just discovered in the previous chapter, Jesus made prayer for the sick part of the mission mandate (see Luke 10:9).

We can also feel, or even be told, that the leaders of our churches must be the only ones to pronounce blessing and that it is a task uniquely appointed for the anointed and appointed elite. We'll return to that shortly but it seems to me that the Bible is a book about a mighty people. When the prophet Joel suggest that the Spirit will be poured out on all flesh there seems to be no suggestion that only a tiny minority will be able to mediate the works of the Spirit to others. The 'mighty man of God' theory of the miraculous stumbles and inhibits many from praying and declaring the will of God for people, places and the land (see Joel 2:28).

Declaring the possibility of blessing for people and households is also inherent in the command from Jesus that the disciples were to declare the peace of God in the form of blessing, and then respond to those who received that blessing and offered welcome (Luke 10:8).

We Bless Because God Blesses

When we look at the meaning and context of the biblical word 'bless' we can define it like this: a multiplication of God's favour resulting in prosperity, fruitfulness and an enjoyment of victory over enemies.

Prosperity is not linked directly to the idea of money as some would have us believe, but speaks of the whole person, body, soul and spirit, prospering and enjoying the favour of God. This will bring prosperity in relationships and strong community. It will strengthen us through the hard times. Clearly God does want to bless us financially but that is only a balanced part of the whole.

Victory over enemies speaks of how God equips us to thwart the works of the principalities and powers at work in our communities and nations. We reign over the works of darkness (aware that our battle is not against flesh and blood) by the word of our testimony (see Rev. 12:11). That testimony includes the declaration of His desire to show mercy, His character and the blessing inherent in declaring His peace for people and places (see Luke

10:5). It serves notice on the demonic strongholds. The Peace-Bringer and His people are here to establish divine strongholds and the powers of darkness must yield to the authority of those who come in His name.

The desire of God to bless us is made explicit when God tasks Aaron to declare His blessing over the people.

> The Lord said to Moses, 'Tell Aaron and his sons,
> "This is how you are to bless the Israelites. Say to them:
>
> 'The Lord bless you
>   and keep you;
> the Lord make his face shine on you
>   and be gracious to you;
> the Lord turn his face toward you
>   and give you peace'.
> So they will put my name on the Israelites, and I
>   will bless them"'. (Num. 6:23-27)

The fruit of the blessing and the favour of God that flows from it is grace, mercy, protection and peace. There will be concrete outcomes. This is not a blessing for nice feelings—it is a blessing for the nitty-gritty realities of life.

God's heart is to bless, and we are called to imitate Him. One of the most shocking aspects of the biblical narrative is God's desire to bless those who do not yet know Him. The promise to Abraham is that all nations will be blessed through him (see Gal. 3:8). The mantle of blessing is eventually taken up by Jesus, who sends His disciples out into the world to disciple the nations.

So how does blessing unfold in the life and teaching of Jesus?

We Bless Because Jesus Showed Us How

Having spent time training and teaching the disciples, Jesus sent them out two by two to bring the kingdom near to people. Jesus' birth had been heralded by angelic choirs declaring blessing:

> Suddenly a great company of the heavenly host appeared with the angel, praising God and saying, 'Glory to God in the highest heaven, and on earth peace to those on whom his favor rests'. (Luke 2:13)

Simeon had blessed Jesus at the temple; this godly man also declared that Jesus would be a sign that would be spoken against.

Blessing would therefore never be far from the lips of Jesus and a declaration of peace would be a key part of the message that the disciples would bring. Despite their evident humanity the task of blessing and bringing healing was being delegated to them.

> When you enter a house, first say 'Peace to this house'. If someone who promotes peace is there, your peace will rest on them; if not, it will return to you. (Luke 10:5-6)

The Hebrew word for peace is shalom. It has multiple meanings which include ideas around peace, harmony, wholeness, completeness, prosperity, welfare and tranquility. Pronouncing it is a comprehensive mission statement in itself. Stop for a moment and think what the seven words above might mean for your home, your street or your town. Think how they expand our vision for mission beyond verbal persuasion. God has authorised you to declare that these things are His will and that they will come to pass in the lives of those willing to receive them.

But Jesus doesn't stop there. A sevenfold blessing is never far from His lips:

> *To the woman who touched the hem of his garment He says*: 'Go in peace and be freed from your suffering'. (Mark 5:34)

> *To the woman who anointed his feet, amidst the seething hostility of the people in the room because He extended forgiveness for her sin, He says*: 'Your faith has saved you; go in peace'. (Luke 7:50)

> *To the raging forces of nature He declares*: 'Peace, be still. And the wind ceased, and there was a great calm'. (Mark 4:39 ASV)

> *To the disciples who will carry on his work He gives this promise*: 'Peace I leave with you; my peace I give you'. (John 14:27)

The promise of a continuing blessing is implicit in his
statement of and offer of peace: 'Peace be with you'.
(John 20:19)

This peace was being offered to all the wrong people. It's a gift to the chronically sick, the morally suspect, the tax collectors, rough-and-tumble fishermen, and other outsiders in Jesus' band of followers. They are all having a sevenfold blessing declared over their lives. Jesus counters the exclusion mentality of His day with the embrace of grace and the promise of peace.

Jesus was so orientated to blessing.

He told His followers that they were to bless those who cursed them. He rebuked His disciples for attempting to block the parents who brought their children to be blessed. This was not an unusual request and Jesus desired to do it. The language of the passage about Jesus' embrace of the child infers the language of adoption. The blessing Jesus gave and the embrace of the child signified the adoption of the child by God and all the mercy, grace and favour that this implied (see Mark 10:16).

He reminds them that blessing comes to those who love the least, the last and the lost. 'But when you give a banquet, invite the poor, the crippled, the lame, the blind, and you will be blessed. Although they cannot repay you, you will be repaid at the resurrection of the righteous' (Luke 14:13-14).

And then Jesus talks of a blessing of power:

'I am going to send you what my Father has promised; but stay in the city until you have been clothed

> with power from on high'. When he had led them
> out to the vicinity of Bethany, he lifted up his hands
> and blessed them. While he was blessing them, he left
> them and was taken up into heaven. (Luke 24:49-51)

He lifted up his hands and blessed them—what is the significance of that? The priests would form a shape with their fingers that symbolised YHWH, the Hebrew name for God. Symbolically the name of the Lord and all the promise of His character is being placed on the disciples.

This would not be the first time that the blessing of God would be marked by the fire of God. Tongues of fire would later descend in the Upper Room and empower the disciples for service.

> Moses and Aaron then went into the tent of meet-
> ing. When they came out, they blessed the people;
> and the glory of the Lord appeared to all the people.
> Fire came out from the presence of the Lord and
> consumed the burnt offering and the fat portions
> on the altar. And when all the people saw it, they
> shouted for joy and fell facedown. (Lev. 9:23-24)

So Jesus is our example. He had limited His majesty to walk among us (see Phil. 2:6-7). His humanity and divinity is held together in a way we can barely comprehend. But in His humanity He ministers and does what He sees the Father doing and very clearly tells the disciples that they can expect to minister in this way and see greater things, despite their humanity.

We Bless Because God Commanded It

We tend to equate the idea of being a priest for God with being an official in the church. But God seems more intent on raising up a people who will bear His image and speak for Him on the earth.

> Now if you obey me fully and keep my covenant,
> then out of all nations you will be my treasured pos-
> session. Although the whole earth is mine, you will
> be for me a kingdom of priests and a holy nation.
> (Exod. 19:5-6)

It is clear that in the goodness of time God set apart the tribe of Levi to ceremonially minister as priests and that Aaron ministered as a priest as we discovered in Numbers 6. It is tempting to then set aside the role of the rest of us as image bearers or envoys for God and accord elite status to the Levitical priest. But that does not seem to do justice to the scripture.

It helps me to think of it in this way. I love playing the piano. I was invited to apply for a scholarship to a famous music college when I was younger but was not ready to give over eight hours a day to practice. I can still play with a small degree of skill and find it wonderful to do so. It can be both relaxing and worshipful. My playing can bring pleasure to myself and others. Together we all admire the highly trained concert pianists but their skill does not negate our own small abilities or stop us playing as best we can.

In our churches there are pastors or ministers who have been set apart to equip God's people for works of service. They have a purpose in the economy of God. But the creativity, insight and service that they bring does not negate the ministry that flows from around the congregation to build up the entire community.

In the epic prophecy of Isaiah 61 that Jesus used to announce His ministry we are told that those who mourn will themselves become those who are ministers of God, priests of the Lord. All of this is in the context of everything that this passage says about material change and restoration in the everyday life of the devoted and the flourishing that will take place.

This idea that the people of God spoke His will and carried His message for the everyday things of life is implicit in the prophetic word.

Elsewhere the psalmist rails against the enemies of God and mentions blessing as if it was a commonplace occurrence.

> May those who pass by not say to them,
>> 'The blessing of the Lord be on you;
>> we bless you in the name of the Lord'.
> (Ps. 129:8)

Blessing motifs were deeply woven into the fabric of life. The peace greeting was part of the social discourse of Jesus' day among the people—it was as if you were requesting God's best for the one you greeted.

Jesus does not negate that tradition but as with much else breathes new meaning into it and applies it to the hard questions and hard situations and indeed the enemies of God that the psalmist felt should be denied a blessing.

We Bless Because It Is the Fruit of a Thankful Heart

God forgives; we forgive. We welcome strangers because we were strangers once. We live out the wisdom that rescued us. Our gratitude to God directs us toward the service of others.

Of course, we cannot separate pronouncing blessings from the acts of blessing through the way we live. James tells us:

> What good is it, my brothers and sisters, if someone claims to have faith but has no deeds? Can such faith save them? Suppose a brother or a sister is without clothes and daily food. If one of you says to them, 'Go in peace; keep warm and well fed', but does nothing about their physical needs, what good is it? (James 2:14-26)

The mere recitation of the words of blessing is not enough. Our life must be oriented toward the attitude and behaviours of blessing.

The same people who God teaches to bless in the Numbers account are warned against polluting the land.

> 'Do not pollute the land where you are. Bloodshed pollutes the land, and atonement cannot be made for the land on which blood has been shed, except by the blood of the one who shed it. Do not defile the land where you live and where I dwell, for I, the Lord, dwell among the Israelites'. (Num. 35:34)

If we are to be imitators of God we must live holy lives, produce works that bless others as well as being those who speak blessings without partiality.

We Bless Because God Has Chosen to Act through His Image Bearers

From beginning to end the Bible is a story of a King and His kingdom. Our future is in a renewed earth. Jesus takes everything captive that the enemy has stolen and gives it back to the Father. We are living in the midst of that story as those who bear something of the image of God.

We are, however, often deeply locked into a pattern of thinking that we must be tentative in prayer in case our request is outside the will of God. We are loath to pray with authority as agents and envoys of the authority of Jesus. We're loath to put on the spiritual uniform that makes it clear that we are empowered to act on behalf of the King of Kings.

I was speaking to a group of Anglicans in the mountains, and in one of the sessions I was introducing them to the ministry of blessing. Having taught from the Scriptures, I said that there was a very big difference between speaking blessing and ministering blessings. I explained the difference between interceding for God to bless and pronouncing blessings.

I invited a lady at the back to come forward and be used as an example. She was quite happy for that. I said to everyone: 'My desire is that this lady here should be blessed'. I wasn't aware at that point that she was the vicar's wife. I then turned my back on her and started to pray. I said: 'Father, You're the God of blessings; I ask you to come because of Jesus, and release mighty blessings on the lady standing behind me. Amen'.

I asked the congregation what I had done. 'You've blessed her', was their response. I said, 'Well actually, no, I haven't; I've petitioned the Father, I've asked Him to bless her. When I as a Christian bless somebody, it's quite different'.

I turned around, faced the woman, and said, 'I bless you in the name of Jesus, that the Father may bless you. I bless you that the peace and the joy of God may come upon you and wash through every part of your being, physically, mentally, socially and spiritually'.

Her eyes filled up a little, she thanked me, and sat down. We carried on and it was only at the end of the day that she came up to me and said, 'Do you know, it's quite amazing, I have suffered from chronic, constant back pain for twenty years and it disappeared the moment you blessed me'.

Our foundations for presence-carrying effective ministry such as this are found in Deuteronomy 10:8. At that time the Lord set apart the tribe of Levi to carry the ark of the covenant of the Lord, to stand before the Lord to minister and to pronounce blessings in His name, as they still do today.

They are for all the people of God, including you and me:

1. To carry the presence of God.
2. To stand (not run, rush) and minister to the Lord.
3. To pronounce blessings.

Jesus takes this up in His ministry. He *stands* in the presence of God through His own drawing aside to pray, noted six times in the book of Luke, and his participation in the synagogue and temple patterns of prayer.

He commissions the seventy-two disciples to minister in the power of the Spirit as He breathes on them and blesses them that the peace of God might be with them (see John 20:22). They will *carry* His presence.

He provokes them toward blessing by His own resolute commitment to it and His inclusion of it in the instruction to *pronounce* peace over the households of the towns He has sent them to (see Luke 10:5).

We are released to the full purpose for which we were made when we carry God's presence, minister to Him in spirit and truth and speak blessings. The power and authority for healing and restoration is released when we speak the words that heaven speaks. When we ask that it might be on earth as it is heaven we are speaking the words that heaven spoke through Jesus.

We Bless Because All of Creation Is Longing to Hear the Heart of God

God cares about the land itself. For instance, Moses speaks of the Promised Land in terms of the Father's promise, comparing it favourably with the arid desert land of Egypt: it is a land sustained by rain from heaven, a land that the Lord their God cares for. The eyes of the Lord are always on it from the beginning to the end of each year (see Deut. 11:11-12).

David, the man after God's own heart, held the earth in high regard, writing in Psalm 24:1 that the earth is the Lord's and everything in it.

One of his most thrilling passages speaks of God blessing the land and of the land's response like this:

> You visit the earth and water it;
>   you greatly enrich it;
> the river of God is full of water;
>   you provide their grain,
>   for so you have prepared it.
> You water its furrows abundantly,
>   settling its ridges,
> softening it with showers,
>   and blessing its growth.
> You crown the year with your bounty;
>   your wagon tracks overflow with abundance.
> The pastures of the wilderness overflow,
>   the hills gird themselves with joy,
> the meadows clothe themselves with flocks,
>   the valleys deck themselves with grain,
>   they shout and sing together for joy.
>   (Ps. 65:9–13 ESV)

God may reveal to us root causes of spiritual issues in our locality. Or we may discover them via natural means such as historical research or observation. We can combine these two in what you might call informed blessing or informed intercession. This helps us 'test the spirits' and not be held captive to the unexamined insights of an individual.

When we moved to Ffald y Brenin we became aware that there was spiritual pollution in the land and district. There were spiritual battles that had to be fought. The forest at the top boundary of the land had been a place of witchcraft. Sacrifice took place there— it was not only a thing of the past. Stepping into the wood was hard—speaking the name of Jesus could provoke an invisible attack that threw you across the clearing.

We cried out to God. We would enter the wood because we believed that 'the earth is the Lord's and everything in it'. We would declare the 'blood of Jesus', which is the only antidote for innocent blood shed there. There is no other antidote. We spent time in prayer and blessed the land for goodness and praise.

One day I sensed a great anointing of the Holy Spirit. I called out to the woods: 'Let everything on this land praise the Lord'. A huge wind rattled through the forest, the trees bent and all over the surrounding area birds rose up. The air was full of their song.

It was not very long before we were told that a decision had been made by the National Park, who had stewardship of that land, to remove the wood. It took them two years to cut it all down and remove it, but as the work drew to a close one of their officials voiced what we believed was a word of truth: 'I don't understand, but it seems like the heavy overcoat over this hill has been lifted'.

We also became aware of a nearby drowning well. In times past it had been used for drowning baby girls. Boys could keep the local farms going and could support the parents; girls would be just another mouth to feed. Those that were not killed would have their teeth removed when they came to marrying age so that their husbands wouldn't be burdened by dentistry costs. Darkness dwells where it has been honoured and the attitudes behind barbarity can linger for generation after generation. We wanted to declare a blessing where a curse had lingered.

In 2 Chronicles 7:14, we read the well-remembered phrase, 'And I will hear from heaven and heal their land'. The fact that the land needs healing suggests that the land can be unwell. Biblically there are several major causes for 'sick land'. They include:

Curses.

> The land is full of adulterers; because of the curse the land lies parched and the pastures in the wilderness are withered. The prophets follow an evil course and use their power unjustly. (Jer. 23:10)

Bloodshed and violence.

> You give shameful counsel to your house,
>   Cutting off many peoples, and sin *against*
>   your soul.
> For the stone will cry out from the wall,
>   And the beam from the timbers will
>   answer it.
>
> Woe to him who builds a town with bloodshed,
>   Who establishes a city by iniquity!
>   (Hab. 2:10–12)

Broken covenants.

> As at Adam they have broken the covenant;
>> they were unfaithful to me there.
> Gilead is a city of evildoers,
>> stained with footprints of blood.
> As marauders lie in ambush for a victim,
>> so do bands of priests;
> they murder on the road to Shechem,
>> carrying out their wicked schemes.
>> (Hos. 6:7–9)

Sin.

> Even the land was defiled; so I punished it for its sin,
> and the land vomited out its inhabitants. (Lev. 18:25)

Unfaithfulness and idolatry.

> They even sacrificed their sons
>> and their daughters to demons,
> and shed innocent blood,
>> the blood of their sons and daughters,
> whom they sacrificed to the idols of Canaan;
>> and the land was polluted with blood.
> Thus they were defiled by their own works,
>> and played the harlot by their own deeds.
>> (Ps. 106:37–39)

All of these lead to judgment and back to the promise of 2 Chronicles 7:14. As we have already noted, we are to do three things:

1. Carry His presence onto the land.
2. Minister to Him from the land and intercede for it.
3. Speak blessings over it.

So we cried out to God. We prayed and we invoked God's forgiveness and the power of the blood of Jesus to take away the present guilt. We spoke blessings into the land; blessing is God's antidote to cursing. We had to declare a new day. We had to proclaim that the peace of God was coming to that place. We had to release the land itself from bondage as we invoked the mercy and blessing of God.

> For the creation waits in eager expectation for the
> children of God to be revealed. For the creation was
> subjected to frustration, not by its own choice, but
> by the will of the one who subjected it, in hope that
> the creation itself will be liberated from its bondage
> to decay and brought into the freedom and glory of
> the children of God. (Rom. 8:19–21)

The plan of God is to reconcile all things to Himself. The promise is that lions will lie with lambs, and the land will flourish. We can be part of the foretaste of that coming day as we bless the land.

> For God was pleased to have all his fullness dwell
> in him, and through him to reconcile to himself all

things, whether things on earth or things in heaven,
by making peace through his blood, shed on the
cross. (Col. 1:19–20)

So we also bless the land. God is calling every aspect of creation back toward the shalom that He desires. This is probably the least recognised ministry of blessing.

Speaking blessings breaks down into three distinctive areas. Speaking blessings over individuals, communities and on the land. So how do we do that?

For further information, visit www.ffald-y-brenin.org, or go to Roy's website, www.roygodwin.org, for additional resources, including study material such as The Blessings Course.

Chapter 7

PRONOUNCING THE BLESSINGS OF GOD

One of our Team members at Ffald y Brenin was chatting with two of the guests in the Common Room. They enquired about healings taking place at the retreat Centre and asked if they could talk more in response to her suggestion that people were often healed. They questioned, 'If it's spontaneous then it's clearly God doing it, but if you were ministering to someone who is sick, what would you actually do'?

She shared some principles before they prodded more. 'If someone was in front of you with broken bones, how would you minister to broken bones'? Sharon was honest and said that was outside her realm of experience but shared what she had often heard us say: 'Bones, we're speaking to you in the name of Jesus and in His name we command you now to be perfectly knitted together'.

This seemed a little brief to them but she explained, 'Usually people are able to come back in a few days without the cast and with a story of how the break can't be found on the X-ray anymore'. She then excused herself and left them for a team meeting.

Later that day she was called to the chapel where the same guests sat radiant and thankful. The woman held her hand up and wiggled her thumb. Sharon was a bit puzzled until the explanation came tumbling out: 'This thumb has been badly injured and immobile. I'm due to have an operation in two days' time. Now I have complete and normal movement in it. It happened when you spoke the words: 'In Jesus' name I command you to be perfectly knit together'.

There was more: 'I broke my big toe years ago and it has been immobile. But it isn't now; it's like a brand-new toe'.

It was a big breakthrough for the lady but also for Sharon, who now felt more confident to minister in the authority that Jesus has delegated to us.

Like her, many of us will step into the arena of blessing and proclamation with some trepidation. Not about what God wants but about what we might say and proclaim.

I was working with some visiting students in a Mediterranean nation. I helped them to think through some questions about the kingdom of God, the locality and the foreign culture and to work out what they might do. Then I took them into a very hot, thriving Mediterranean market place. It was huge, incredibly smelly and crowded with people. They walked and walked up and down the streets and around the stalls and through the market. Here is some of what we pronounced:

I bless the very land that my feet touch in the name of Jesus.

I bless this place in the name of Jesus that this community, this land, this foundation on which a community is built may give glory to Jesus.

I bless it as the creation of God, filled with unseen redemptive purpose.

In Jesus' name I bless the feet that will walk over this land, that some of them may be those who develop beautiful feet that carry the peace and the blessing of Jesus.

There were crowds of people walking toward us—we blessed their families and their circumstances. Among them were many young people—we blessed them that from amongst them there may be raised up mighty leaders for Jesus.

We were seeing what was possible for God, with whom nothing is impossible. We didn't understand their language and they didn't understand ours, but as we invoked blessing we were doing meaningful work for the King of Kings in that place and amongst those lives.

A Basic Structure to Our Blessings

As we consider how we might construct a blessing, it can be helpful to think about the three key building blocks of blessing.

1. I bless you ...

The prophet Isaiah reminds us that:

> The Sovereign Lord has given me a well-instructed
> tongue,
> to know the word that sustains the weary.
> He wakens me morning by morning,
> wakens my ear to listen like one being
> instructed. (Isa. 50:4)

As we come to pronounce the desire of God to bless, the power is not found in empty words but in the response of God to our proclamation as one who has been given delegated authority. It's not that our words are magic, but that they carry authority if we are in the right position.

In the corner of my room is a rather fine—although unusual—seat, and there is a story involved. Daphne was leading a blessings team close to the English border and had stayed in a home where the husband was a retired craftsman. She commented on a rather unusual seat and he explained its background. Meanwhile, two thousand miles away and unaware of Daphne's conversation, I was talking with the Lord about the practice and exercise of authority, and sensed Him saying that He would teach me more when I arrived home.

When I returned Daphne started to tell me about her trip and surprised me by saying that we had been given a gift of a chair. She then explained the background; the man had been producing perfect replicas of what had been called in Roman Empire times 'the Seat of Authority'. It was collapsible; a magistrate might go to the centre of a town and his servant would carry the seat, complete with Roman emblem.

As long as the magistrate was on his feet he was no more than a Roman citizen; however, the moment he sat in the seat of authority his words carried the full force of the Emperor himself. Once he left the seat he was no more than a man amongst men.

We were given one of the replicas complete with historical provenance. Other copies are in London museums and with the Royal household. I learned so much and thanked the Lord. I am seated with Christ in the heavenly places, and so are you as a believer. His name is our 'seat' in terms of authority. Found in Him, we can speak normal words that are clothed in all of heaven's delegated authority. That's where we need to be when we bless.

The Bible refers often to calling on the name of Jesus or praying in His name. It is part of the wider story where the people of Israel call on the name of the Lord. It could take many pages and indeed books to explore what this means but it can also be summarised in this way.

When we pray in His name we are calling on the promise of His character. We are asking Him to come and 'hallow' His name by releasing the fullness of who He is into our lives and of those around us, causing Him to be called holy. We are leaning on His mercy and compassion. Part of the promise of His character relates to His authority—He is the King of all kingdoms, part of our commitment to Him is that we call Him Lord, and we recognise no other ultimate authority. So in speaking in His name we are coming with His authority to address all that is broken or in need of renewal in the life of people, communities and land.

2. That He …

My words in themselves are unlikely to carry the power to change people's lives. The name of Jesus, on the other hand, carries all authority. So when I bless, it is in order that He might break in and confirm the words with signs following. That's how the Lord explained the ceremonial blessing to Aaron: Say the words and put My name on the people, and I will come behind you and bless the people.

If we were to say to a deaf person that we blessed them they might thank us. On the other hand, if we were able to say 'we bless you in the name of Jesus' we would have invoked the promise of the Lord to come and do wonderful things in that person's life. If we were to say 'I bless your hearing' I can't imagine it having much effect, but we see the effect of blessing deaf ears in Jesus' name repeatedly. They open so often!

There are unending opportunities to drop a bomb of blessing into someone's life, family, into places, regions and so on. Sometimes the gifts of the Spirit mingle and we might bless like this:

I bless you in the name of Jesus that your eyes may be so transfixed on Him that other things that want to take your eyes in other directions may fall away. That you may gaze upon His beauty; that you may have eyes for nothing but Him. That you may be transfixed by the One who looks at you and says—you keep looking at Me and I'll keep looking at you.

Be aware that sometimes there is an immediate response, but for others there might be an unfolding over minutes, hours, days or weeks. God gently and mercifully goes behind their defences and starts a work. Some will need to repent. In blessing them we are not blessing their deeds, we're blessing them for change.

3. May …

One way to look for models of blessing in the Scriptures is to hunt out the word 'may'.

Psalm 20 offers a good example of scripture that we can use to speak blessing over people as it contains the word may—used not in a tentative sense but in a strongly positive 'this is what God desires to do' way.

May the Lord answer you when you are in distress;
> may the Name of the God of Jacob
>> protect you.

May He send you help from the sanctuary
> and grant you support from Zion.

May He remember all your sacrifices
> and accept your burnt offerings.

May He give you the desire of your heart
> and make all your plans succeed.

May we shout for joy over your victory
> and lift up our banners in the Name of
>> our God.

May the Lord grant all your requests. (Ps. 20:1–5)

It's a great section of Scripture to turn into a blessing. For example:

In the name of Jesus, I bless you, that He may answer you in the day of trouble and that He may do it so clearly that you may know without any question that it's Him.

You see how we do it?

I bless you in the name of Jesus that the name of the God of Jacob may protect you. That you may be safe—that you may be secure. I bless you that He may send you help. I bless you in the name of Jesus that He may grant your heart's desire and fulfil all your plans. As I bless you, I promise that I will shout for joy over your salvation.

I bless you that the Lord may fulfil all your petitions; that everything you cry out for, everything you seek may be given to you by the One who loves to say … Yes!

We should be eager to bless.

I believe that God wants to give you a redemptive revelation so that you dream His dreams. That revelation will then inform how you pray and increase your faith for what God will do. He wants you to see how things could be in the life of people, places and regions. He wants you to imagine their redeemed future and then pray blessing for them in the light of that.

What's the size of the canvas on which we might dream dreams and see visions? Because in general the size of our canvas, the size of our imagination sanctified by God, is what will determine what we might expect and ask for. This is partly why the book of James says you don't have because you don't ask (see James 4:2-3).

There is so much more that we could actually ask for, but the size of our imagination has limited the canvas of God's activity. That's going to be affected by the stories we've heard; the culture we've grown up in; the things we've already experienced of God; our experience of local church and so on.

If we only know that God occasionally helps somebody with a headache to feel rather better, we might be a bit stunned to discover that He is also able to make a limb grow, for instance, because we haven't got a canvas that big. It's not God who is limited, but He will work with the framework that we will allow Him to work within.

In the Old Testament we discover that God is able to do more than we could ask or imagine. If that is so, wouldn't it be great if God touched our imaginations and enlarged that canvas and made a fertile ground in which faith really could truly respond and believe?

There has to be a conversion of our thinking. There has to be a revelation of God's word to our intellect, our mind and understanding that allows us to take off the spiritual glasses we're wearing and put on another pair with different lenses which give a much larger and wider view. I recently had my eyes tested and then I had a new pair of glasses made. Almost immediately I ran into problems with headaches and pains in my eyes.

I went back and was told that the nose pads needed resetting and that my glasses weren't quite in the right position, so they corrected all that. I went back a month later and told them I thought they'd moved again and they reset them. And so it went on. In the end they re-tested my eyes and they discovered that they had the wrong lenses.

When I received the new pair of glasses with the right lenses, I suddenly found that I had comfort in my vision that I hadn't had before. As well, I had a full range of vision instead of the almost tunnel vision that I had with the initial pair.

It's exactly the same thing with our spiritual perception: God can come and do something with our minds that changes the way we think. We see the Scriptures differently when we read them, and see a larger focus instead of a smaller one. Then God speaks to us and it stirs faith and we can imagine so much more and therefore we can ask for so much more.

The Message Bible's version of 1 Peter 3:8–9 captures something of what working with a redemptive revelation might look like:

> Summing up: Be agreeable, be sympathetic, be loving, be compassionate, be humble. That goes for all of you, no exceptions. No retaliation. No sharp-tongued sarcasm. Instead, *bless—that's your job, to bless.* You'll be a blessing and also get a blessing.

To whom might you show mercy? How might you cultivate good? Acts of blessing work alongside words of blessing. The mercy of God lifts a weight off us completely. We are encouraged to cast our cares upon Him. By extension our small acts of compassion for others—gardening, transportation, a listening ear, simply having mercy in the face of difficult behaviour are both acts of mercy and acts of blessing. We do them with no agenda, not asking for anything back. But they are an instrument of the Holy Spirit, a means of grace and more often than not they provoke people to ask about Jesus.

Redemptive Revelation for People

Whenever we pray for people we need to see the whole person. I heard a story once of a man taking an art class. They were painting a planter box, a fairly simple object, and our friend quickly finished. The art teacher sent him back to his easel and asked him to look at the box again from a different angle.

This happened several times and initially sparked a bit of annoyance. But after a while my friend realised how much richer his understanding of the play of light on the box was and how much better he understood what it meant to paint something that truly captured what he was seeing.

We referred earlier to the shalom prayer of peace that Jesus commissioned His disciples to pray (see Luke 10:5). The word *shalom* is rich in meaning. As you think about speaking blessing over someone you might want to think about what the following words linked to shalom might mean in the life of that person. It may soon become clear what you should pronounce in the light of that person's circumstance:

> Peace
> Harmony
> Wholeness
> Completeness
> Prosperity
> Welfare
> Tranquility

So you might bless with respect to harmony:

I bless you in the name of Jesus that you may know a strengthening of relationships, restoration of broken friendships and fruitfulness together as friends.

There is a common-sense wisdom that also prevails when we speak blessing. Imagine that you are blessing someone with a respiratory infection:

I bless you in the name of Jesus that your total respiratory system might be cleared through, that He may cause your immune system to rise up and that your sinuses may become clear.

There will always be an element of simply waiting on God and listening for a prompt from the Holy Spirit as to what would be appropriate to speak; or we may sense or see in our mind's eye the blessing that He has for a particular person or people. God gives us a gift to deliver to somebody else.

Do we only think of gifts in individual boxes? As we think about praying blessing we should be sensitive to the fact that God may give us discernment, a word of wisdom or a word of knowledge. Any of these may aid us as we pray.

In the midst of it all we act with sensitivity and without manipulation. Sometimes God wants us to ask a question and not make a statement. A friend travelling on a plane got a very strong impression about the male passenger next to him. There was an issue in his life with a woman called Sally. Later in the journey they got into conversation and my friend eventually asked him: 'Who is Sally'? The man was in shock—nobody knew about his mistress, least of all a stranger on a plane. But he had been asked gently and without confrontation. So they were able to talk about the issues the man needed to address.

The blessing acrostic can help direct us into well-rounded areas for blessing:

- **B**ody—health, protection, strength; God wants to restore us and renew our health.
- **L**abour—work, reward, security; because God cares for the whole person.
- **E**motional—joy, peace, hope; health here means health in the rest of our life.
- **S**ocial—love, marriage, family, friends; we were created for community.
- **S**piritual—salvation, faith, grace; God desires to renew us in the patterns of our thinking about Him, our purpose in the earth and our future hope. Whoever we are, believer or non-believer— He wants us to discover the mind of Christ.

You can also think about what that acrostic might mean for places and it is to these we now turn.

Redemptive Revelation for Places

When God established Abraham in Canaan He told Abraham to explore where He had sent him.

> The Lord said to Abram after Lot had parted from him, 'Look around from where you are, to the north and south, to the east and west. All the land that you see I will give to you and your offspring forever. I will make your offspring like the dust of the earth, so that if anyone could count the dust, then your offspring could be counted. Go, walk through the length and breadth of the land, for I am giving it to you'. (Gen. 13:14–17)

God instructs him to walk the land. What was Abraham doing as he walked the land; claiming, praying, thanking, dreaming, blessing? Probably all these things and much more beside.

We were approached and asked if we were willing to draft a form of blessing that could be used to interlace the Welsh/English border, an area with a complex history. We were pleased to do so. Numerous temporary Houses of Prayer were established along both sides of the border and Daphne walked almost 190 miles as she led a team to carry the blessing between them, which was then spoken out across the border. This is what was proclaimed:

Wales/England! (Depending on which side of the border they were)
We bless you in the name of the Lord.
May you be blessed by the Lord, who made heaven and earth!
May you be blessed in the town and blessed in the country,
In your going out and in your coming in.
May the spirit of salvation fall upon your people
And may you be overtaken by joy.
May you rise up in your destiny and give glory to God!
We bless you, our neighbour, in Jesus' name!

Soon afterward a newspaper reported that the local government on both sides had agreed to work together for the economic and social improvement of the cross-border regions. Coincidence?

In 2012 the Olympic torch was carried by relay across the United Kingdom ahead of the London Games. I was invited to produce a form of blessing which could be used in tandem with the torch run and spoken out across the UK as well as at the Games themselves. This is what I produced:

I/we stand in the mighty name of Jesus and bless you, (place/region), that you might prosper under the mighty hand of God.

I/we bless you that justice and righteousness might take their proper place within your boundaries. I/we bless you that the favour of the Lord might rest upon you and give you peace.

I/we bless you that the Father's compassion might fall upon your people. I/we bless your poor that they might be lifted up.

I/we bless you that the knowledge of Jesus might come in amongst you like a flood.

I/we bless the people of God in this (place, region), that they might rise up with Servant authority and become a people of blessing.

I/we bless you that the joy of the Lord might be your strength.

There were stories of significant and immediate impact from across the country and some athletes or Christian Workers sought permission to translate it and take it home with them to use there. The London Olympics were widely reported as 'the friendly games'.

A people of blessing will make it their practice to walk the area that they have a heart for. What might you dream for that area? What might be your 'redemptive revelation' for that place?

You can walk the area and imagine what it is going to be like when His will is done on earth as it is in heaven. Imagine these people worshipping together. Imagine brokenhearted people healed; broken families restored; imagine salvation coming; imagine future hope released. As you walk you will start to notice things more and God will spur you to pray for and to bless in new ways for the local community.

This outward-looking, other-directed faith that seeks to see people through the eyes of Jesus is formed by habits of the heart, which are cultivated by the rhythms of grace we intentionally commit to. What are those rhythms?

For further information, visit www.ffald-y-brenin.org, or go to Roy's website, www.roygodwin.org, for additional resources, including study material such as The Blessings Course.

Chapter 8

HOW GREAT A SALVATION

It was a New Wine clergy day (a gathering of pastors involved in Holy Spirit renewal, often in Anglican/Episcopalian churches). I was introducing our time together and told everyone I was going to teach, model, and practice what it meant to pray for others to be healed. After the initial Bible teaching we moved toward the practical demonstrations. I had a word of knowledge about someone in the room with a damaged left knee. I told the group what I believed God had said to me and said that we would pray for that person in a public way as a demonstration and model of what God desired to do.

I looked around the room to see if anyone was indicating that they were the person with the problem knee. I thought I saw a hand quickly raised and just as quickly hidden away. I asked the seemingly reluctant lady if we could pray for her. 'I don't see the point', she said. 'I have been prayed for so often and nothing happens'.

I love hearing that. Some find it depressing to hear the lost hope that lies behind those words. I can understand why that might be so. But it makes me think about all the prayer that's already gone on for that person. We then get to join in at the end.

She agreed to be prayed for, however, and with some difficulty made her way to the chair on the platform. It was clear just how misshapen and damaged her knee was. I asked her to tell us a little more. She had undergone many operations and some bones had been rotated during various surgeries. If you stood close enough you could see the scars through her stockings of all the work that had been done.

I invited people to stand or gather near the front so that they could see exactly what was wrong with the knee as I began to command it to change shape in the name of Jesus. We waited and the knee began to change shape and size. The next step was to bless what God was doing and start to deal with the pain issues.

She had told us that she was in constant pain. When she had attempted to move her knee earlier the gasps of pain and discomfort and grind of bones could be heard by all of us. We commanded the pain to go in the name of Jesus. She indicated that there was an immediate and significant lessening of the pain.

There were some in the meeting that day who had been somewhat skeptical about healing but now they witnessed with their own eyes the changes in her knee and heard her testimony to a release from pain. She moved her leg around and experienced no resistance. She stood to walk and the grunts of pain and other noises from her knee were heard no longer. There had been a wonderful healing.

For the church leaders there were perhaps mixed feelings. They had observed the word of God in action. The kingdom of God had been demonstrated. But it raised the question: had they just witnessed that particular lady being healed, or was there a deeper principle being shared? This was about God's desire to bring in His kingdom, including the release of compassionate healing and mercy.

Let's examine something of the flow of biblical revelation.

> He said, 'If you listen carefully to the Lord your God and do what is right in his eyes, if you pay attention to his commands and keep all his decrees, I will not bring on you any of the diseases I brought on the Egyptians, for *I am the Lord, who heals you*'. (Exod. 15:26)

Here in this verse we find God declaring His character and His purpose. 'I am the Lord who heals you'. This is the active voice of God. He is not reflecting merely on His past attributes or interaction with the people, He's talking about Himself now and in the future.

The words of the psalmist and his majestic declaration of the character and intent of God further reinforce this:

> Praise the Lord, my soul;
>   all my inmost being, praise his holy name.
> Praise the Lord, my soul,
>   and *forget not all his benefits*—

> *who forgives all your sins*
> > *and heals all your diseases,*
> who *redeems your life* from the pit
> > and crowns you with love and compassion,
> who *satisfies your desires with good things*
> > so that your youth is renewed like the eagle's.
>
> (Ps. 103:1–5)

Part of the challenge we face is that we often find ourselves listening to the idea that we shouldn't ask God for anything—that we should only seek His face but not His hand. Actually, God wants us to seek His face and *also* seek His hand. He wants us to examine how we view Him and let our beliefs shape our attitudes and our consequent behaviour.

As we reflect on healing we may feel that there are problems in our lives which will be a barrier to healing. We may be consumed with guilt or concerned about character issues in our life. But the Scripture is very plain in what it promises. It tells us that God will heal our diseases. The placing of love and compassion on our heads then speaks of the renewing of our mind so we might think with the character of God as a guide and have the 'mind of Christ'.

It can be tempting to view God as an 'errand boy to satisfy our wandering desires' (Bob Dylan) on the one hand or feel guilty for desiring good things on the other. We may be tempted toward resignation if we believe that everything that happens to us was predetermined by God before the beginning of time and that we should therefore find a way to cope with our circumstance. But the psalmist seems very clear. God desires to renew us.

The Prophet's Challenge

God often speaks of salvation and healing in the same breath. If we dismiss the idea that He will heal now we'll have to take a scalpel to the passages where healing and salvation go hand in hand.

Healing is a form of salvation activity; it is a part of our redemption. In Christian culture we can come to believe that God is only concerned about our spirit. We start to believe that our bodies and our minds and the environment we live in are of little concern to us or God. All that matters in this view is that one day we will go to heaven. This is not actually a scriptural portrayal of the good news of God expressed in Jesus.

> Surely he took up our pain
>   and bore our suffering,
> yet we considered him punished by God,
>   stricken by him, and afflicted.
> But he was pierced for our transgressions,
>   he was crushed for our iniquities;
> the punishment that brought us peace was on him,
>   and by his wounds we are healed.
> We all, like sheep, have gone astray,
>   each of us has turned to our own way;
> and the Lord has laid on him
>   the iniquity of us all. (Isa. 53:4–6)

As a young Christian I was always taught that the passage referred to our sin and rebellion and had nothing to do with physical healing.

I do not believe this to be true and here is why. The Gospels explicitly see Jesus as the fulfillment of this prophecy.

> When Jesus came into Peter's house, he saw Peter's mother-in-law lying in bed with a fever. He touched her hand and the fever left her, and she got up and began to wait on him.
>
> When evening came, many who were demon-possessed were brought to him, and he drove out the spirits with a word and healed all who were ill. *This was to fulfill what was spoken through the prophet Isaiah*:
>
> 'He took up our infirmities
>   and bore our diseases'. (Matt. 8:14–17)

Jesus was working out His Messianic manifesto before their eyes. John the Baptist also believed that Jesus was sent from God. But he had a slightly different vision of what should happen when the Messiah came. So he sent his messengers to Jesus to ask if He was indeed the One. Jesus responded:

> Go back and report to John what you hear and see: the blind receive sight, the lame walk, those who have leprosy are cleansed, the deaf hear, the dead are raised, and the good news is proclaimed to the poor. Blessed is anyone who does not stumble on account of me'. (Matt. 11:4–6)

The essence of who Jesus is finds expression in the things that He does. Go and report what you see and hear is what Jesus encourages the disciples of John to do.

> Great crowds came to him, bringing the lame, the blind, the crippled, the mute and many others, and laid them at his feet; and he healed them. The people were amazed when they saw the mute speaking; the crippled made well, the lame walking and the blind seeing. And they praised the God of Israel. (Matt. 15:30–31)

The future hope is becoming a present reality in Jesus. He has brought the kingdom. We begin to touch now in the present the beginnings of what will become total on the day when Christ returns. You cannot separate healing from the proclamation of salvation, the good news of the King.

> As you go, proclaim this message: 'The kingdom of heaven has come near'. Heal those who are ill, raise the dead, cleanse those who have leprosy, drive out demons. Freely you have received; freely give. (Matt. 10:7–8)

The peace, healing and wholeness and restoration mandate of Jesus is made explicit as He sends the disciples out for mission and kingdom bringing. They have seen Jesus at work, they have listened to His teaching; now is the time to put it into practice. Like Jesus, they will be utterly dependent upon the Father. He delegates His authority to them, breathing on them to impart the Holy Spirit. Then He instructs them:

> When you enter a town and are welcomed, eat what is offered to you. Heal those there who are ill and tell them, 'The kingdom of God has come near to you'. (Luke 10:8–9)

The testimony of Jesus was at work in the life of His disciples. They did not spend protracted time trying to work out whether God would heal. They simply acted in the authority that Jesus had given them.

> Now a man who was lame from birth was being carried to the temple gate called Beautiful …
>
> Then Peter said, 'Silver or gold I do not have, but what I do have I give you. In the name of Jesus Christ of Nazareth, walk'. Taking him by the right hand, he helped him up, and instantly the man's feet and ankles became strong. He jumped to his feet and began to walk. Then he went with them into the temple courts, walking and jumping, and praising God. (Acts 3:2–8)

> Nevertheless, more and more men and women believed in the Lord and were added to their num-ber. As a result, people brought those who were ill

into the streets and laid them on beds and mats so that at least Peter's shadow might fall on some of them as he passed by. Crowds gathered also from the towns around Jerusalem, bringing those who were ill and those tormented by impure spirits, and all of them were healed. (Acts 5:14–16)

God did extraordinary miracles through Paul, so that even handkerchiefs and aprons that had touched him were taken to those who were ill, and their illnesses were cured and the evil spirits left them. (Acts 19:11–12)

Let us examine for a moment the authority of Jesus.

When Jesus had finished saying these things, the crowds were amazed at his teaching, because he taught as one who had authority, and not as their teachers of the law. (Matt. 7:28–29)

Let us be clear. Jesus is the author of life. He speaks with authority because He speaks the Father's words for creation. Matthew then reminds his readers throughout chapters 8 and 9 that it was not merely the Father's words that Jesus came to declare but it was the Father's works in creation that Jesus came to demonstrate. As we seek to understand the ministry of blessing and our role in proclaiming life, grasping hold of Matthew's litany of miracles and what it says of Jesus' authority and intent is part of discovering the backstory of blessing.

On what basis does the leper come to Him seeking healing and from where does he get his confidence? 'If you will you can make me clean'. He recognises the authority of Jesus. Jesus' response is immediate. 'It is my will, be clean'. The healing happens.

What prompts the centurion to ask simply for a word? Jesus said to him, 'Shall I come and heal him'? The centurion replied, 'Lord, I do not deserve to have you come under my roof. But just say the word, and my servant will be healed'. He recognised the authority. The centurion knew about authority.

Faith has arisen, as a response to the revelation of the authority of Jesus. It comes by hearing, grasping or being seized by the word of God in all of its different expressions. Intellectual response to Scripture is important but it is not enough. We need to take hold of the message and let it renew the patterns of our thinking and temper the stormy waves of our emotions.

What has God breathed into you? What is His word for your present circumstance? Seeking healing on the basis of proof texts is not what we pursue. That leads to presumption about the power of words or formula. We need a revealed word to provoke faith. In an earlier chapter Rachel had a dream about her healing—faith was released in her. There is nothing wrong in coming forward in hope for healing but coming forward in faith is better still.

We learn through the five senses God has given us. We get all kinds of cues from things other than speech. But love and especially His love are outside those five senses. They might all contribute. We can see the evidence of God working, but we need faith and revelation to believe He will work in our lives. What we receive from God is received by faith.

Let us be clear about the desire God has to bless, renew and heal because it is against that backdrop that blessing, mission and the presence of God, the kingdom, comes on earth as it is in heaven.

> When Jesus came into Peter's house, he saw Peter's mother-in-law lying in bed with a fever. He touched her hand and the fever left her, and she got up and began to wait on him.
>
> When evening came, many who were demon-possessed were brought to him, and he drove out the spirits with a word and healed all who were ill. (Matt. 8:14–15)

Think about Jesus' ministry for a moment. Leprosy is gone, paralysis is gone, fever is gone with a touch. The authority of Jesus is very clear. Jesus is the same yesterday today and forever. All authority in heaven and earth has been given to Him. He took our infirmities, lifting them off us so that we might be healed.

But His authority is more extensive than physical healing. He calms the storm. His disciples are afraid. But He rebukes the storm. His authority is being expressed in every sphere. He later heals the man let down through the roof. He also tells him that his sins are forgiven—a challenge to the religious observers who believed that only God had that power to forgive. Jesus once again states His authority.

Jesus at that moment also makes it clear that there is a new arena that the Holy Spirit is going to work in. Everyday people will soon do extraordinary miracles in ordinary places. Ordinary people will pronounce forgiveness, blessing, healing and wholeness. The glory of God was going to dwell among the people. God was going to 'tabernacle' in everyday people. We were going to be the new temples.

> Do you not know that your bodies are *temples of the Holy Spirit*, who is in you, whom you have received from God? You are not your own. (1 Cor. 6:19)

Jesus reminds His hostile critics:

> 'Which is easier: to say, "Your sins are forgiven," or to say, "Get up and walk"? But I want you to know that the Son of Man has authority on earth to forgive sins'. So He said to the paralysed man, 'Get up, take your mat and go home'. (Matt. 9:5–6)

Jesus reminded them that His authority exercised in the healing stemmed from His authority as the Son of God and that He could both heal and forgive.

Much of this book is about taking hold of the scriptural patterns for our lives that we find in these accounts of the life of Jesus. We're seeking to understand how we might imitate Jesus. We may feel that we are mere audience members in the theatre of God's salvation but He wants to delegate His authority to us, making us to be actors for Him in the divine drama. If we will just take hold of His Word and declare it over dying or broken bodies, bitter and divided nations and the places where He has called us to live we might see extraordinary things, perhaps the reality of things we have dreamt of.

What authority has He given us and how can we take hold of it? Are these things merely the things that Jesus did or should we expect that we could see God at work through us? Jesus seems very clear.

> Very truly I tell you, whoever believes in me will do the works I have been doing, and they will do even *greater things* than these, because I am going to the Father. (John 14:12)

Greater things. Think about it. Greater things!

But we never walk alone in the Way of Blessing—so what does God want to say to us about a community of blessing?

For further information, visit www.ffald-y-brenin.org, or go to Roy's website, www.roygodwin.org, for additional resources, including study material such as The Blessings Course.

Chapter 9

A COMMUNITY OF BLESSING

One of our volunteers answered the reception door to find a man standing there who was very excited and very keen to speak to me. I went to the door and we greeted each other. The man kept shaking my hand and wouldn't let go. He explained: 'I just want to thank you so much. You've changed my life and you've saved my marriage—I just want to thank you so much'.

I had never met him before and gently suggested that I didn't think I had the power to change anyone's life, and certainly not to change anybody's marriage. I invited him to tell me his story.

He explained how miserable his life had always been. He got married and demanded that his wife produce a good breakfast every morning for him, and how it never satisfied him. Every morning he would criticise her by saying how it wasn't presented properly or cooked correctly. He would look at what she was wearing and criticise that too, along with her hair.

He criticised his neighbours. He criticised his friends and lost them. He struggled to keep jobs because he criticised everybody—his co-workers, the bosses. They would get rid of him. He would go somewhere else and do the same thing.

He became a Christian and he criticised everybody and everything. He very quickly found that in a local church setting he could easily gather a group of people around him and show them very quickly from the Scriptures why the leadership were wrong and weren't doing what God wanted, creating cliques and eventually he would be thrown out. This happened at several different churches. This attitude of his had shaped his life.

Somebody gave him a copy of *The Grace Outpouring*. He was stunned by what he read about blessing and thought maybe he could try that. The next morning his wife produced his breakfast and he thanked her, ate it and told her he really enjoyed it. He told her she looked lovely. This threw her into a bit of a panic—she wondered why he was being so nice to her and it became a bit of a mystery and a threat for a while.

He began to talk nicely to co-workers in his job and he found that he could easily get people together at work and show them how effective the bosses and managers were and how in difficult circumstances they were doing a brilliant job. Now he was favoured because he encouraged and strengthened all the people around him.

At church, he began to find that he could easily gather a group of people around himself and show them from the Scriptures how excellent the church leaders were and urged them to speak well of them and to pray for them and respect them. Suddenly he became very valuable as a member of the body of Jesus.

And then he found that he could look at strangers and without thinking about it say, 'Father, help me now' and then speak blessing on them in the name of Jesus for a revelation of God to be upon their lives. He told me: 'It's got to the point where I can walk down the street in the town where I live and see a stranger walking toward me and I don't have to think about it—I can't help myself; I just bless them under my breath the moment I see them. It's my first reaction. But until this recent development I had never understood that all my previous life I have walked in curses'.

I tell this story because it is so encouraging but also because it captures something of what makes a community of blessing a reality. This man's perspective on people, the work of Jesus and the place of blessing was shifted as he read *The Grace Outpouring*. It made a difference straightaway in all the communities that he touched—home, work, church and the wider local community.

As his understanding of his role in the purposes of God was nurtured, the fruit was relational. If we are to be a community of blessing that declares the blessing of God for people, regions, communities, and the land, then we have to wrestle with how we bless each other by words and behaviour in the mundane everyday things of life.

The Impossible Community

Jesus' twelve disciples are a good example. They were both a small community themselves and a community that leaked into other communities. Peter took them all round to his house and they had a meal and simply spent time together.

But if truth be told they are the impossible community. You've got the tax collector betraying his people by acting for the occupying army. You've got the zealot who wants to attack and throw out the occupying army. How impossible is that? Imagine Jesus calling you to follow Him and you do, but a mile down the road you see His gaze fall on somebody else whom you are not fond of at all—and He invites them to come and live with you!

This impossible community is not going to work unless Jesus is at the centre of it. It's socially impossible and it's unlike any other community on earth. Being part of a community of faith does involve us with living with people who get on our nerves; who frustrate us; who irritate and annoy us, and even drive us to distraction. And that is exactly the kind of community that God is drawing us into.

Sometimes we think that the ideal Christian community will be wonderful; everybody loves us and gets on well with everybody else. But actually, God draws us into community to knock us about, to allow us to be hurt and struggle and to find our feet and to have lots of our rough edges knocked off in the process.

This impossible community is there not simply to be observed; we are called to be part of it and to closely fellowship with those in it, even though it feels like a building site, covered with scaffolding and muddy puddles and awkward bends and turns and materials that don't really stick together very well. That imperfect community is there to say to those outside, come on in. In its imperfection, it is very good news for people. They can come in their brokenness and join in the process of being healed.

God's purpose is to produce community. Paul tells us in Colossians 1:20 that the Father wants to reconcile all things to Himself through

Jesus. That starts in and spreads from the communities of reconciliation we find ourselves in. Our impossible communities are the body of Christ; they are not necessarily homogenous in that they contain a whole mix of people, histories, views and cultures that couldn't possibly live together unless Jesus was really at the centre.

When this redeemed community arises within a city, town, village, neighbourhood or network something quite startling and different to what is already at work in that community will be taking place.

Held Together by Jesus

Our Christian communities don't always function in the way that I am describing above—in other words, there's a gap between what we would verbalise and probably believe and what we actually do. For all sorts of quite natural reasons it's easy to be centred on our past story, our roots, or our particular spiritual emphasis—but not centred on Jesus.

New Christians often grasp this Jesus-centred perspective instinctively but sometimes we have to work at it with people who we sense have drifted into a lifeless orthodoxy. There's a good litmus test for this in any Christian fellowship, whatever size or style it might be: where do your resources, time and energy go? Often they go into supporting our programmes, our missions, all sorts of things. These are things we should be doing; but they're not the things we should be centred on.

The prime thing we should be doing is being centred on Him and worshipping Him. Our prime focus should be that. This then becomes part of our intentional reflection together and starts to shape the songs we sing, the prayers we pray and the scope of what we read and study. Within our Morning Prayer is the prayer of St. Patrick:

> Christ as a light illumine and guide me. Christ as a
> shield overshadow me.
> Christ under me, Christ over me, Christ beside
> me, on my left and my right.
> This day be within and without me, Lowly and
> meek yet all-powerful.
> Be in the heart of each to whom I speak, In the
> mouth of each who speaks unto me.
> This day be within and without me, Lowly and
> meek yet all-powerful.
> Christ as a light, Christ as a shield, Christ beside
> me on my left and my right.

The community of believers spurs each other on to understand more of the life of Jesus. Meditating on His story equips us for the storytelling we do out in the world. It informs the pattern of our thinking. It shapes our heart attitude and provides an opportunity for the Spirit to bring us insight and revelation.

Our Christian communities are one of God's favourite signs of the kingdom. They point to the kingdom and witness about the kingdom.

There are some things that enhance that community that we have found helpful.

Learning to Listen

One of the things that we have learned at Ffald y Brenin is to listen to one another, rather than cut across one another to put over our point of view, but rather really listen to one another. To listen to that difference of opinion and to accept that the person who holds that opinion is likely to do so entirely sincerely. We value their right to hold their own opinions sincerely. We may challenge their opinion, but what we would never do is challenge the person.

For me personally that's something that took me quite a long time to understand and much of my pilgrimage in this understanding came through our diverse team and our diverse guests here at the Centre.

I had been somebody who prided himself on logical, analytical thought. Who would bluntly say to absolutely anybody: 'I disagree with you'. I simply didn't understand how difficult and how painful I often made those conversations for other people. I've had to learn to say to myself: *Actually it's not that I disagree with the person; it's their viewpoint or belief that I find difficult.*

And I can avoid saying: 'I disagree with you', and instead say, 'It's interesting because I would see it quite differently. Tell me why you would feel so strongly about that subject'.

I have had to learn to shut up and listen, and let people express themselves. And then perhaps say: 'Can I explain why I see it a little bit differently'? and then gently open up the situation. Do not go charging into the discussion with the person you disagree with and verbally attack them—even though often it's not what you mean to do. The truth is, that you don't like it when somebody comes and verbally attacks you over your views.

When you are committed to community your personal change creeps up on you and you look back and are reminded of how much you have changed. The disciplines of living in community and teamwork make you more of a listener. You find that you have two ears and one mouth and you need to use them in that order!

There is a constant throughput of people at the Centre who express every possible idea and theology under the sun. You can often see the pain and the loss that people live with because of an erroneous understanding of the Scriptures. They've been taught something—this is what you believe as a Christian—which is simply not true and if they knew the truth the truth would set them free. You feel compassion for rather than frustration with people. Compassion gives birth to gentleness and you seek to impart the truth with grace and dignity.

Having become a community being shaped by the kingdom of God and its values we then turn toward our wider communities.

Infecting Our Communities with Blessing, Love, and Service

One day Daphne said that she had been invited to take a Blessings team to speak one evening in Selsey and had accepted. The invitation came because they had read *The Grace Outpouring* and decided to experiment by blessing their town.

'Good', I said, 'and where exactly is it'? We looked it up and to her amazement found it to be a town around 270 miles away cross-country on the south coast of England. Daphne was surprised by how far it was but was sure that she should go, even if there were only a few people there for the meeting.

Off they went and met some nice local believers. She shared with them about the ministry of blessing. They took her and the team to see a shop in the town, which they felt the Lord might be giving them, and Daphne blessed it.

Some time later they invited her back. It so happened that I was due to be travelling in that direction so we both visited and what a joy it was to see what God had done. We started off in the town hall with a joint churches meeting where, after a time of worship, one of the men read out a list of blessings received since a cross-church group started to minister blessings to the town.

It started with, 'The fishermen in the harbour are reporting much bigger catches'. He then mentioned the way that the shops and restaurants had each independently cleaned and decorated the frontages, how churches were working together in the town, civic groups were functioning better, and then he said, 'and of course we have the golden buses'.

Golden buses? I was intrigued and asked for more detail. Apparently the county council had some exceptional public buses joining their fleet. Apart from colour, they boasted stitched leather seats and free Wi-Fi. They could have gone anywhere but they were awarded to Selsey. Then new lights were put on the roads and a thorough re-surfacing took place.

Robin, who testifies of all this, said that the scripture 'the rough places shall be made smooth' came to mind. But there was more; when winter floods hit, their area of Selsey was not flooded—as it usually was. Plus, a local wealthy businessman decided that what Selsey needed was a nice sandy beach, so he built one!

We left the town hall and went to see the shop, now imaginatively named 'SHOP'. I was rather surprised until they explained that it stood for Selsey House of Prayer. People are able to drop in for a coffee and perhaps a chat whereupon they may be invited to receive a blessing.

The favour of God seemed to be on the town with people making choices that were good for everyone. But the people of God were also bringing blessing to the everyday area of their relationships. It might not always be in their physical neighbourhood but in civic life, shop-front prayer stations and work undertaken together they were demonstrating the kingdom and declaring the blessing of God. We have to move beyond words and prayer however.

Love Is an Action

We had moved and I was just beginning to lead a particular congregation some years before our time at Ffald y Brenin. We were talking about love, and I asked them if they believed that as Christians God loved them. They all said yes. I asked if they believed that they were called to love others. They said yes again. I asked if they loved everybody in their community and everybody in their fellowship. They said yes again.

I asked if they really believed that they were called to do this. I said and what about so and so, who has been a member of this congregation for so many years, ever since he was a toddler and is now a mature man. He's had his electricity cut off and his water and telephone cut off because with the industrial cuts he was laid off and hasn't been able to find work. How have you loved him then?

I could see that it stopped them in their tracks, because love isn't a feeling in the New Testament sense. Love is an action. How do we know that God loves us? It isn't because we experience warm emotions. This is how we know God loves us: He sent His only Son. Love is something that you do. How do we know that God loves us? He came and rescued us.

Being part of the Christian community enhances our witness. We can resource together to be larger and more visible. So as a Christian in my daily life (just in the *flow* of my daily life), because I have been loved by God, I find my attitude toward others constantly changing. I find it easier and easier to be compassionate and to love people, including those I would naturally find quite unlovely. And that's because God has loved me, and I'm learning to love them.

So we learn to love and we learn to serve people. We don't seek to lord it over others any more, because Jesus came and served us. So our attitude is different. We might give; we might work for a local drop-in centre or a soup kitchen or just help someone in whatever practical way we can, because we are being changed into those who serve from the inside out.

We bless wherever we can bless. We bless by both pronouncing blessings and wherever we can by being a blessing. We bear witness by the way that we live and then by naming the name of Jesus.

Let me say that again. We bear witness by the way that we live and then by naming the name of Jesus. So often we have reversed that order and created a barrier that is too big for people to leap over. They need to see that we are all right before they listen to our message and consider whether God is all right. How will they know we are trustworthy, full of integrity, unless our living matches our words? We walk the talk.

When we come together in community, we can do all this multiplied by a factor of X. We can resource more and there's more we can do together. There are ways that we can go out and be a blessing on a larger scale and be more effective than when we are simply on our own.

We can do so much more together. It has always been God's redemptive plan to build a new people, a royal priesthood and a holy nation. That's us.

Minister into What You See

When it comes to our church communities infecting the wider community with the presence of the kingdom of God and the works of the kingdom of heaven it can be useful to walk our neighbourhoods with a desire to bless in the name of Jesus and to listen to what God might tell us via our eyes, ears and our willingness to listen to Him stirring our hearts.

Some time ago my sister-in-law rang Daphne and said. 'You know I have the *Methodist Recorder* every week, which is the denominational weekly. I can't believe it—the whole of the front page and the inside of the front page is all about *The Grace Outpouring*. It's all about blessing'.

There were impassioned denominational conversations going on big enough to fill the first three pages of the weekly denominational broadsheet. The call was this: what would happen if the people called Methodists said that their prime calling in the twenty-first century was to be particularly a people of blessing, who pronounced blessing, and poured out blessing wherever they are. The Methodist Conference said they wanted to pursue this and employed someone for twelve months to put the subject on the agenda of their United Kingdom churches.

There's a challenge there that I would like to offer to all Christian communities: what would happen if they would corporately become a people who consciously blessed, who were open to the blessings of God, but who received more and more blessings because they were pouring out intentional blessings wherever they went.

As we walk around in the natural flow of the things we need to do, around our towns or neighbourhoods, we can often discern the spiritual patterns or forces at work in people and communities. The dark side of this is that we can fall into a pattern of judgment. The challenge for us is: are we going to do the walk of judgment or the walk of blessing? Will we actually look at our society from a grace perspective rather than a judgmental one? It's a massive challenge for many of us because our whole mind-set, from varying theological perspectives, is the other way, one of exclusion, judgment and even anger.

What would a kingdom community perspective bring to our daily walk? What would the walk of blessing embrace? Let's consider one model …

Responding to the Words of Jeremiah 29:7

> Also, seek the peace and prosperity of the city to which I have carried you into exile. Pray to the LORD for it, because if it prospers, you too will prosper.

You can quietly speak out these blessings as the opportunity arises. You could also walk with one or two others in a planned walk. Bless conversationally as you walk together. Bless with humility—large groups with arms raised aren't quite what is needed for this type of ministry!

At a school:

We bless this school in Jesus' name that it may be a secure and safe place for teachers and pupils. We bless the children's capacity to learn and play and develop relationships. We bless them to have an opportunity to hear about Jesus and His love for them. We bless them to grow like a mighty oak tree for the nations to see and marvel. We bless this place that those who lack hope will find shelter here from the storms.

Restaurants and eating establishments:

We bless all those who work here in Jesus' name that they may offer welcome, hospitality and community. We bless this aspect of life in the town and ask that it will continue to be a good means of income for many. We bless them as they give hospitality and welcome to others. We bless them that they might discover Jesus who loves feasts, banquets and a table of welcome.

A main square, market place, town centre or shopping precinct:

We bless this place in Jesus' name and the markets and trading that take place here. We bless those who work here that their businesses might prosper and bring value and service to the lives of the people of this town. We bless the conversations which take place here. We bless those who honour Your name that their mouths will be full of wisdom and truth for those conversations. We bless in Jesus' name that the sense of community around these streets would continue to grow.

By a pharmacy, surgery or hospital:

We bless the health of the people in this locality in Jesus' name, that they may be strong and well. In Jesus' name we resist any sickness or disease which seeks to invade this town and to every person here we say, be strong, be healthy. To any who are sick right now we bless you in Jesus' name that you might enjoy a speedy recovery.

At a church:

We bless all the Christians in the town in Jesus' name, those who are part of a congregation here or who meet with other Christians elsewhere, that each one may be like a light shining out for all people to see. We bless the Holy Spirit gifts of the Christians in this place, and that He may flow like a river through each one of them.

By courts, police stations, probation offices or places of rehabilitation:

We bless those who keep watch over the safety and integrity of the town in Jesus' name. We bless those who also seek to ensure that there is justice for all that their voices might be heard. We bless those who seek to restore those who fall and fail. We bless your church that it might be part of this process.

The town hall:

We bless all who live and work here and around the town to ensure that life is well ordered for all who live here in Jesus' name. We bless them that they would promote beauty, joy and provision of good things for all who live here and that these things would be part of the heritage of the town.

From Our Hillside to Your Town

In the business world people often talk of pilot projects. In the software world they talk of beta software. These early versions help creative people learn lessons and correct problems. Then what they have done is released to everyone.

For several years now the Way of Blessing that has been impressed on us has moved from the 'pilot project' or beta stage and begun to touch other communities across the United Kingdom and around the world. How has the Holy Spirit moved hearts, provoked pilgrimage and established new 'thin places' around the world?

For further information, visit www.ffald-y-brenin.org, or go to Roy's website, www.roygodwin.org, for additional resources, including study material such as The Blessings Course.

Chapter 10

SURPRISED BY THE HOLY SPIRIT: AN UNEXPECTED MOVEMENT OF BLESSING

All that you have read thus far is set against the backdrop of a small retreat centre in the heart of Wales. We have learnt much about the *Way of Blessing* as God has taken us on an adventurous journey at Ffald y Brenin. But God has bigger plans for revival and restoration than one Welsh hillside alone. So we've quietly been seeking to impart to others the truths that have shaped us, and out of that desire was birthed the *Local Houses of Prayer* movement.

For a number of years we have held an annual conference for those who are engaged with what we call Local Houses of Prayer. One early delegate was Jill, a remarkable Christian woman from

Norwich, many miles from us, in the east of England. She was very excited about the principles and possibilities we outlined and the colonies of blessing that might arise as a result.

She and her friends had found favour among many churches and were given a redundant church in the very centre of the city, close to the cathedral, to use as a physical expression of a House of Prayer. It blesses and resources churches from across the city for prayer, blessing and the mission that flows out from that.

It also serves as a living model of what is possible as it has sparked the growth of a large network of Local Houses of Prayer that have been raised up across the city and further afield, in the local county and beyond. They now also work closely with the ministry of Sozo (from Bethel, Redding) so that when the hurting and wounded come into the House of Prayer, believers or unbelievers alike, they are able to minister to them very clearly and simply and see God bring healing. It has been a marriage made in heaven.

Another delegate from a training day, Heather Read, emailed us after a few weeks with an invitation to a rural setting near Poole in the southwest of England. It was an area made famous during the '70s and '80s by the presence of a Christian community which was the centre for the Fisherfolk, a Christian worship and recording group, and for the ministry of Jean Darnall.

Heather was seeking advice, help, and encouragement. It's quite a distance to travel because they're also at the end of miles of country roads and lanes. We got in contact and found that she had already established twelve Local Houses of Prayer. We couldn't remember who she was, but we decided to go!

Heather had arranged for local people who were involved to come together for a light early evening meal and a question and answer time.

There was to be an open meeting a little later to talk about Local Houses of Prayer to anyone who was interested in learning more. It was a beautiful early summer evening and it was unusually warm and the meal had actually been quite big; the sheer size of the pizza was memorable!

Suddenly, Phil, her husband who is also a pastor of the church, rushed in and told us we needed to stop the current informal meeting. There were well over one hundred people standing outside in advance of the open meeting! There was consternation because the church didn't hold that many people in addition to the numbers already inside!

So, there was a lot of to-ing and fro-ing and people ended up sitting on the floor in the Sunday school room and in the kitchen. Doors and windows were open hoping that people would hear, as I shared with them and taught a little about Local Houses of Prayer. We encouraged them to stay in contact with Heather and to attend a training day.

A little while later, she contacted me to say that she was concerned about how she could manage so many emerging groups. I suggested that she look for people who were rising up from amongst those who were involved who could be the overseers for five groups but still attend their own Local House of Prayer. That's what she began to put into practice, but as for those new overseers—some of them are running with the vision and planting nearly as many as Heather has.

I have been going back on a regular basis to the Lighthouse Church where hundreds of people have come together and we have seen the Holy Spirit move in continuing power with freedom and healing and deliverance.

Local Houses of Prayer are an integrated model for equipping radical believers and releasing God's blessings on earth. Their focus is: 'That the manifestation of the kingdom of God might be powerfully released right here where we are'.

I'll not tell you the whole Local House of Prayer story or outline all of the foundations that undergird it in this chapter right now. But here are some of the core tenets.

A Local House of Prayer is not simply a house where some people pray. There is much more going on than that. It is not a house group, a Bible study or a pastoral group.

In essence, two or more people have a desire that the kingdom of God, that is, the rule of God with revelation, justice and salvation, should break into the lives and circumstances within their own community. What 'community' means here will depend on the lifestyle of the people involved. It could be their home streets and neighbours, or where they study or play, or even a virtual online network, which has become their personal community.

Individually they will commit to spending a small amount of time on their own praying for a small number of identified people in a particular way and with an accompanying blessing. Outlines, help and teaching materials are available from Ffald y Brenin but it is best understood by attending one of the many Local House of Prayer Training Days, which take place across the country and in many nations.

Each day we reflect on some of what we call the Caleb Questions. (As we discussed in length in chapter 4, Caleb was an Old Testament biblical character who stood out from amongst the people around him by his single-hearted commitment to follow the Lord, and he received an inheritance of answered prayer.)

- Who or what is God putting in front of you that you can affirm and bless?
- Who is God putting in front of you to whom you can show mercy?
- Who is God putting in front of you with whom you can share the Gospel of the kingdom?

Notice the repetitive 'who is God putting in front of you'. The whole point is that we come to understand that the Lord really does intend that you, as well as I, should open our eyes and see what He is doing around us and that we should be the bearers of illuminating truth that leads others to acknowledge Jesus as both Lord and Christ. The Jesus who is the Light of the World also tells His stunned followers that because of Him they are also to be carriers of that same light (Matt. 5:14).

Preferably once weekly, but definitely no less than once a fortnight, the several people meet together in one place (of good reputation):

- They cleanse and dedicate the place for the purpose God has for it—just as we do at Ffald y Brenin.
- They seek the manifest Presence of God each time they meet.

- They are building an altar in their community; that is, there is a pattern of identification, worship and sacrifice. The sacrifice is the surrender of their own lives to the service of God and the community.
- They long for the reconciliation and redemption of all things, both in creation and among the people that God created.
- They stand together in unity—agreeing with heaven and each other that the people they are praying for should be saved.
- They both bless and intercede, with an individual, community and land focus.
- They believe for the breaking in of the kingdom, the rule of God in our communities.

The group would also reflect together on what we call the fuller Caleb Questions:

- Who or what is God putting in front of you that you can affirm and bless?
- Who is God putting in front of you to whom can you show mercy?
- Who is God putting in front of you with whom can you share the Gospel of the kingdom?
- What opportunity is God opening up for you as a group, to declare the good news of the kingdom in your area?

- Who is God putting in front of you whom you
  could invite to come and join with you?

Churches, movements, and cross-denominational groupings
are using this pattern of individual and group practice. As well,
individuals are being used to penetrate the lost lives or unreached
communities around them.

So, it seems as though the movement of Local Houses of
Prayer has become infectious. Another aspect of the unexpected
movement of God relates to the growth of prayer houses around
the Mediterranean. We have quietly sought to encourage this but
sometimes even the stories we hear take us by surprise. One captures
both the growth of Houses of Prayer and God stirring up His people
across the nations.

As a result of reading *The Grace Outpouring*, Martin, a YWAM
leader in a European nation, contacted me. This nation like several
in Europe is a culturally Greek Orthodox environment. Many like
me have found many helpful insights within the Orthodox tradition concerning the Holy Spirit, but in the day-to-day realities of
life things can be hard for non-Orthodox believers in those nations.
I felt I should respond to him and the desire of his team to establish
a House of Prayer.

On the plane over I read a long email from them that had just
arrived. It seemed they did not actually have a House of Prayer or
even a present form of one. In my humanity this made me a bit
grumpy. I had carved out some costly time from a busy schedule
just before Christmas! This frustration melted away as I met the
team and discovered their heart and their desire to see a House of

Prayer established that could impact the whole of their nation and the region as well.

After a few days together we went away to a rustic retreat where I shared some insights and facilitated their capturing of their own vision. When I taught them concerning the Way of Blessing they did not find it easy to practice; as with many people their instinct was to ask God to bless, rather than bless people themselves in the name of Jesus, using the authority God has given us.

I rushed home in time for Christmas with our family. As the New Year started the team commenced a House of Prayer, initially using Martin's front room. They began to pronounce blessings over the area. In their second week something extraordinary happened in a local school a couple of miles away.

Late one evening a twenty-nine-year-old teacher had felt prompted to change her Facebook page so that it mentioned she was a Christian with a relationship with the Lord Jesus. The next morning when she went into school, two of the girls from her class went up to her and asked how they could know Jesus in the way that she did. She was stunned. There were a number of thoughts that hit her. The first one was: *What are my eight-year-old pupils doing looking at my Facebook page?* The second was: *What are they doing looking at it at midnight?* Thirdly: *I could lose my job over this!*

She quickly prayed and told them to see what they thought the next day. If they were still interested, she would explain. The next day she arrived at school to find her whole class waiting in the playground so that they too could know about Jesus. She told them to quieten down and to go into the classroom, and she went in and did the attendance register.

Then, after a breathed prayer, she talked to them about a Saviour, Jesus, who was so wonderful to know—she explained the ABCs of salvation through Jesus. But she warned them and stressed some of the difficulties that might arise for them from the conventional religious authorities. Even as eight-year-olds, they could be in very serious trouble with their families and with their community for deviating from the national religion. She really stressed that it was a very big commitment indeed and there was a cost to be counted if you became a follower of Jesus.

She said that they were going to have a few minutes of quiet time and asked them to think about what she had said very seriously. She told them that they could even discover that their brothers and sisters would never speak to them again and stressed that it was an enormous step to take. She told them that they mustn't make the decision unless they had really thought it through.

She took a while and let them have time and then said she was going to pray a simple prayer to Jesus and if they had really thought it through and understood that their whole life might be affected by this decision, that they could pray quietly using the words she was saying.

She finished the prayer. There was no *Amen,* just silence. The children sat there in silence. She thought that they may have thought the risk too great. But suddenly, the children erupted in shouts of praise.

That evening she thought about the fact that she hadn't mentioned the Holy Spirit, so she called a local pastor she knew whom is also a friend of ours. She told him what had happened and that she hadn't mentioned the Holy Spirit. She asked him if he thought she should, and he reminded her that the work of the Spirit is also part of the gospel. She thought: *I'm going to lose my job, but I'm going to lose it for the whole class, so …*

She completed the register the following morning and then told the children she wanted to talk to them about the Holy Spirit, whereupon the Holy Spirit came rather like the day of Pentecost in Acts 2. Some of the children fell on the floor and started worshipping in a new language that God had given them. Some started prophesying with amazing words that God had given them.

Some saw pictures as Jesus ministered to them. Others jumped onto their seats and started shouting loudly the name of Jesus, while some rushed for the chalk to write extraordinary and extravagant praise to Jesus on the blackboard! The whole classroom was in a tumult, which was when the door opened and the deputy head walked in! The teacher felt her job would soon be terminated.

She walked around the classroom without disturbing what was going on and stood next to the deputy head. He said: 'There is trouble here. This means such trouble'.

Yes, she thought, *this really does mean a great deal of trouble for me.*

But to her surprise, he explained: 'In my teens I heard about Jesus and I laid my life down and surrendered it to Him, but after a short time, I discovered all the things that the world had to offer and I made a very deliberate choice to turn my back on Jesus. From then on I have chosen to take everything I can. I have walked in sin and pleasure throughout my life, and now I'm in trouble. God is here—what do I do?'

So she directed him to the pastor who had helped her the previous night and who was able to help the prodigal return.

Well, the Holy Spirit kept filling the children and they were going out into the playground and prophesying over other pupils. Of course they wanted to share the good news with their brothers and sisters and parents—who wanted to know what on earth was going on.

The news got through to the headmaster and he called her in. He said: 'I believe God is moving in your classroom. You must understand that there are not many schools in our nation that can say: God is actively moving in my school—so you must recognise and honour God and you must do everything He tells you to do.

'We must never become a school that is known to have disobeyed God. It doesn't matter what He says, just do it! The children are eight years old; they can catch up educationally if necessary, but you must always do the attendance register and you must obey God. The timetable is in your hands, but you must obey God'.

Time went on and some parents made a response to the good news of Jesus. Some brothers and sisters did also. At times the children go out into the streets of the town and share the good news with the people in it. They are unstoppable.

This happened during only the second week that the House of Prayer had commenced as they were interceding for the kingdom to come and were proclaiming blessings over the area including their nearest town, which is where the school is.

The essence of what God has been doing with us finds different expression in different parts of the world.

The Far East

A young woman who had a serious skin disease asked us to pray for her. She showed us her neck, arms and feet, and said the rest of her body was also like that. The whole of her skin was crimson and purple as though it had been scalded or scorched. She asked for ministry and we rebuked the disease.

Within twenty-four hours her neck and arms were visibly clear and she explained that the rest of her body was equally whole. She showed us her feet, which now looked slightly bruised, but all the previous purple discoloration had disappeared. We were able to bless them and command the completion of her healing.

She then took out her mobile phone. Just before she asked for prayer the previous day she had taken a picture to show her condition at that time. As we looked at the picture it was clear that God had done the most wonderful miracle here.

But this was not at Ffald y Brenin. It was at a church summer camp meeting for 1,000 people held in a hotel in Malaysia hosted by a Singapore church called Cornerstone.

While we rejoice over the people whose hearts have been touched or repaired, or whose understanding of the goodness of God has been increased, the physical healings that you see are like illustrations and encouragements that help you to know that you should keep going and doing what you do.

We were there because of a man who had been given a copy of *The Grace Outpouring* by relatives in the United Kingdom as he left them to fly home. Once on the plane he realised that he had left his reading glasses behind. He picked up a newspaper and a book but couldn't read them. Then he noticed that, strangely, when he looked at *The Grace Outpouring* he could read it easily. He was impacted by what he read.

He's an influential man and amongst his friends is Pastor Yang, the pastor of Cornerstone Community Church in Singapore, a church of around 4,000-5,000 people. He encouraged him to read the book. Having done so, he quickly introduced it to some of his leaders. They decided to fly to the UK and visit us as soon as possible.

So they did. Unfortunately they didn't call ahead and they just turned up! Daphne and I were ministering in another nation at the time. But they weren't disturbed by that at all. The senior pastor went to the high cross and had what he calls a very powerful encounter with the Lord.

On the journey between the airport and Ffald y Brenin were the remains of the original Bible College of Wales founded by Rees Howells, a famous intercessor, who exercised an exceptional and fruitful ministry, particularly during the time of World War II. The story of his life is famously conveyed in the book *Rees Howells, Intercessor* by Norman Grubb, and had been a top seller for decades. It was a book that greatly impacted Pastor Yang some years previously. He was taken there to see the remains of the college.

To his amazement, as he stood there looking at the remains, he sensed God saying: 'I want you to redeem it'. It was for sale for some millions of pounds, yet amazingly his church raised the money. People who will never be able to visit Wales to see it gave generously as the Lord moved them. They purchased the site and then went on to restore it.

They have opened up a public visitor centre because there is a historic heritage there for Wales, and in fact for the nations. They completed the current phase and honoured Daphne and me at the opening; if it hadn't been for *The Grace Outpouring* none of this would have happened. Later in 2015 they commenced short-term college courses with a prevailing prayer, holiness and missions focus.

By then we were flying over each year so that we could speak at Cornerstone Church in Singapore. There are multiple services because of the size of the congregation and very substantial leadership devolvement to help give pastoral care to such large numbers, with several hundred house group leaders in operation. It is always a huge thrill to be able to speak there and see God move, touching people and opening hearts.

But that was not all. The book handed to the man in an airport was to bear more fruit yet. He shared the book with others in Singapore. They visited the Centre and brought gifts of money, jewellery and clothes. They sat down with me and said they wanted to explain why they were doing this.

'God has shown us that He is going to create a new awakening in Wales and when that happens it's going to trigger awakening in many nations, including Singapore. In many ways our spiritual destiny is waiting on what God is going to release through Wales. So we've come here with gifts like the wise men, simply to honour you and to give into the seeding of the work that God is going to do'.

It was a very humbling and wonderful time. After a few days they left. God had really spoken to one of the men about the nature of Ffald y Brenin. Subsequent to their visit, he, together with some friends in Singapore, restored a heritage building and built a conference centre and retreat hotel inspired and influenced by Ffald y Brenin. It's called Changi Cove.

It is situated in the former British Royal Air Force Far East Headquarters in Singapore. The central heritage building is called Command House—that was the military name, and that is the hub of this remarkable place. People are coming from across Asia and the world to be there. Changi Cove has been built with a spirit of excellence. The restored Command House with its expanse of a parade square and privacy is larger than the separate conference centre and adjoining hotel. The common refrain of guests is one word: 'Peaceful'.

As I was shown around on my first visit, a staffer walked by and my new friend, the man who read *The Grace Outpouring* on the plane, said to me: 'He's a medical doctor. He felt called here and he's given up his career to run this place and even wait on tables'. He was not the only one who had given up position and career development to come and love and serve the many guests and discover that they are being overwhelmed by the peace and sense of presence. It's a remarkable and wonderful work, and although it doesn't look anything like our own modest retreat Centre, they talk of Ffald y Brenin as its inspiration to create a peaceful place for rest, reflection and restoration.

We See a New Africa

Several years ago I was invited to speak on the outskirts of London to a very substantial gathering of people. I was pleased to go and after quite a difficult start to the service itself, God really did break through and do powerful things. As I was surrounded by people at the end and was ministering to them, a visitor had been trying to get through to me to talk but was unable to do so. He found Daphne and explained that he was a visiting pastor from Uganda and really wanted to know whether we would both be prepared to go to Uganda and speak at his church.

It was to be a while but eventually we went. He invited me to a conference in the church where he was bringing together quite a number of pastors from the outlying area. So Daphne and I went, but we also took Anne DeLeyser, the Local House of Prayer network leader from Oxford who has strong personal connections in Africa through the Christian relief organisation, TearFund. She came with us but took off very soon for the Rwandan border area where plans had been made for her to teach about Local Houses of Prayer.

Over the coming week they had an amazing adventure. People were coming up to her and saying: 'Can you tell me how I can become a follower of Jesus? The local team travelling with her were amazed about what they heard about Local Houses of Prayer as she taught and told stories of what God can do.

The church where Daphne and I spoke during the week was quite a small church, but they had gathered about sixty-five pastors from outlying places in the district. They lay on the concrete floor at night to sleep and a fire was lit with brushwood on which maize was cooked, so together with some vegetables there was a meal for them every day. These poor people seemed to glow and were so hungry to know the Lord.

So the week was fine, but there was a sense that we were missing something, a sense that in God's plans we hadn't travelled all the way to Uganda just for this alone. The day arrived when we were flying back to the UK. The plan had been that Anne and her team would come to the hotel where we were staying and pick us up so we could go out for lunch and a debrief before heading off to Entebbe and the overnight flight home.

They were so full of stories that they couldn't stop talking. It was thrilling for Daphne and me to listen to them. They were still interrupting each other with excitement as we pulled up at a compound with big steel gates and an armoured guard. The gates were opened and we were allowed in and the team were still pouring out their stories about what they'd seen God do.

We walked into a very substantial building, and they were still telling their stories. Then somebody appeared and started to take us on a tour of the building, which was full of offices. I was concerned about my lunch and a little puzzled!

A really smartly dressed professional young woman arrived and asked if I was Roy; she informed me that the meeting was going to start in ten minutes, and would be held in the board room.

At that point Anne suddenly remembered that she had forgotten to tell me that they had received a phone call on their journey asking if we would divert and go to the main headquarters of a particular denomination because the main man wanted to have a personal meeting with me. She didn't know why.

A line of very distinguished and sober-suited-looking men came in, along with a giant of a man, who asked if I was Roy. He sat down next to me and explained who he was and told me I had ten minutes to talk about Local Houses of Prayer.

He explained that he had been attending a Pan-Africa Congress that was taking place in South Africa. The night before our meeting God had appeared to him in a dream, and told him that he was to leave immediately because He had brought somebody to Uganda to tell him about Local Houses of Prayer.

God had told him: 'Through their release in the nation I am going to reawaken the spiritual life of your denomination and reconnect you to the Head. You have been wonderful servants, reaching out your hands to the poor and needy, but in doing so you have neglected Me and lost some contact with Me. This is going to be My vehicle to awaken your denomination and to reach out into Uganda afresh'.

So he had flown back, having given his apologies. He contacted his team at home and asked if anybody knew anything about some people who had come into their nation and were talking about Local Houses of Prayer. Nobody knew anything, but someone said that some of the serving team had indeed gone to the west of the country with a visitor to teach about something called Local Houses of Prayer. Through that we were found. This was a God appointment. We didn't actually talk about Local Houses of Prayer; we just talked about the Lord and His blessing and then the Holy Spirit came powerfully upon us with some force and we had a great time.

Anne has become the Lord's voice for us in Africa. She speaks Swahili, which rather amazes the rest of us, but our training material and videos are available now in the majority of the key languages that are used in Africa as well as in the West.

Nations across Africa are expressing an extreme desperation that networks of Local Houses of Prayer should be established. They are grouping together by geography and language in order to facilitate sensible training and we are responding by sending Anne. At her first African national training of facilitators for mission, people came from other neighbouring nations as well and that has repeated itself thereafter. Denominations and streams are working together.

Some of the substantial denominations actually have national facilitator networks and they come together and Anne is able to go out to them. Some of the people who are now running Local Houses of Prayer in African nations travel with her and speak out of their own experience. Even as I write these words, Anne is back in Africa to lead a training course for central and western Africa.

A Holy Spirit Infection

We are struggling to keep up with the number of nations from around the world who are requesting training for large-scale networks of Local Houses of Prayer; some are patient but others are extremely impatient! Daphne was busy founding a new network of Local Houses of Prayer in Alaska last year; testimonies are received from Local Houses of Prayer in the main USA. We keep receiving stories of networks arising across European nations; later this year I will be training leaders in Southeast Asia and Australia.

There is a small but steady stream of emails that arrive at Ffald y Brenin from people across the nations who have visited us, speaking of the way they were impacted when they were here, and how they are beginning to establish new Local Houses of Prayer within their own nations.

So much of what goes on at Ffald y Brenin nowadays is not known by us, simply because of the sheer number of people. We also try to ensure we have a culture at work where no one is expected or required to come and share their story. We want to give them the space to have a confidential encounter between themselves and God. By far the majority of the stories that we do hear nowadays are from outside of the Centre, typically when we are travelling and meeting people, and they both surprise us and bring great joy.

I want to repeat the Caleb questions again as a provocation to you as you finish this story of the work of God among us.

- Who, or what, is God putting in front of you that you can affirm and bless?
- Who is God putting in front of you to whom you can show mercy?
- Who is God putting in front of you with whom you can share the Gospel of the kingdom?
- What opportunity is God opening up for you as a group, to declare the good news of the kingdom in your area?
- Who could you invite to come and join with you?

Glory to God alone.

For further information, visit www.ffald-y-brenin.org, or go to Roy's website, www.roygodwin.org, for additional resources, including study material such as The Blessings Course.

SHARE THE ADVENTURE WITH US

We hope that *The Way of Blessing* has been an encouragement and a faith-building read for you. We know that for some it will simply have been a helpful book. For others it may stir a desire to continue to explore these themes and connect with other resources and events that explore the nature of blessing, mission and the presence of God.

As we sought to follow as closely as possible the pattern that the Lord has given to us, we became aware that many people want to partner with us financially, sowing into this growing ministry, giving rise to 'The Friends of Ffald y Brenin'. Many others have asked how they might identify with our ministry, values and way of life more clearly and walk more closely with us.

For a number of years we resisted any idea of a 'Ffald y Brenin Community', but when several years ago we began to mention it, we found ourselves overwhelmed by the sheer number of people who said 'yes please' from all around the world and so delayed any progress.

We have thought carefully over the years about our capacity for communication, how much commitment we desired from people to our ethos and how we might give away the message that God has delivered to us whilst being wise stewards, guarding the integrity and values evoked by the reputation of Ffald y Brenin.

The fruit of that reflection is what we outline below.

We have launched The Caleb Connection as a supportive network of friends who would like to find a way of sharing together in our values and mission. This finds a focus in our annual June conference, which explores the lessons we are learning, the insights gained and experiences of ordinary people living out the Way of Blessing so that others may enter into it more deeply themselves.

We are also planning to significantly increase the breadth and depth of available resources for individuals and for ministries, where for instance a local church would like to 'plug in' with us.

As the stories of grace are multiplied, more and more people want to visit Ffald y Brenin and while we rejoice at their hunger for God, we are also concerned for those who are closer in relationship with us but cannot find opportunity to stay on-site because we are always so fully booked.

For that reason, we have announced that several weekends each year can only be used by our Caleb Connection friends on a first come, first served basis. There may or may not be some optional input from a member/s of the team, but primarily they are times reserved for you to come and stay on-site on personal retreat. They are not mini conferences (at this time).

Visit www.ffald-y-brenin.org and www.roygodwin.org for more information and resources.

Our Mission

To live transformed lives, secure in the Father's love and pouring out blessings; to go further out into our communities with prayer-based mission and service, particularly remembering the poor.

Our Values

These are only a sample:

- Responding to the invitation of Jesus for us to be with Him
- Living relationally
- Experiencing our life as a pilgrimage
- Learning from kingdom history
- Participating in the Father's purposes

Our Way of Life

These are only a sample:

- To pursue the King and bring worship to Him
- To be thankful
- To seek the kingdom first
- To live a life that embraces simplicity and focus
- To renounce power and manipulation as a means of getting others to do what you want
- To proclaim blessings

A booklet is available online which explains all this in fuller practical detail.

We welcome and appreciate prayer for:

- Ffald y Brenin and its team
- Roy and Daphne's ministry
- Wales via our pray4wales ministry
- The planting of Local Houses of Prayer in the UK and abroad
- Our international ministry

You could also:

- Adopt our values and principles as part of your own life/ministry ethos
- Share in our daily Rhythm of Prayer
- You can support Ffald y Brenin by giving regularly and thereby becoming a Friend of Ffald y Brenin
- You can attend a regional Local Houses of Prayer Training Day

We will:

- Communicate with you regularly and clearly, sharing encouragements, items for praise, and items for prayer.

- Pray for you on a regular basis (please be aware that we cannot offer pastoral care)
- Give you priority booking for our annual June conference at Ffald y Brenin
- Reserve several weekends a year just for Caleb Connection participators

Finally ...

We welcome you to share with us in an amazing adventure as we keep our eyes on Jesus and pursue Him for all He is worth.

Roy, Daphne & Team

To discover more and become part of The Caleb Connection, visit www.roygodwin.org and www.ffald-y-brenin.org.

CONTACT INFORMATION

For further information and resources, including The Blessings Course, please visit www.roygodwin.org.

For more information about Ffald y Brenin and its ministry, please visit www.ffald-y-brenin.org.

The Ffald y Brenin Trust
Pontfaen
Fishguard
Pembrokeshire
Wales, United Kingdom
SA65 9UA

Email: admin@ffald-y-brenin.org

Released in August 2016

LOCAL HOUSES OF PRAYER

A transformed life
A transformed community
by Roy Godwin

In this book, Roy Godwin—Director of The Ffald y Brenin Trust and founder of the L-Hop movement—describes the principles and practices of simple, Biblical steps which can revolutionise your life, your neighbours' lives, and whole communities, as the kingdom of God is powerfully manifested right where you are.

It is hard to believe the speed of expansion of the global phenomena called Local Houses of Prayer (often abbreviated to L-Hops). Particularly when it has poured out to the nations from a little House of Prayer / Christian Retreat Centre in the remote southwest of Wales, UK.

Who is this book for? Roy says, 'If you want to see the Kingdom of God break out in manifest power around you, this book is for you'.

Visit www.roygodwin.org for more information.

The Caleb Initiative in association
with The Ffald y Brenin Trust

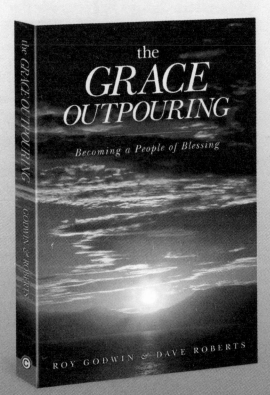